GARDENING IN THE SOUTH

— with —

Don Hastings

FLOWERS, VINES, & HOUSEPLANTS

Previous Books by Don Hastings:

Gardening in the South: Trees, Shrubs, & Lawns
Gardening in the South: Vegetables & Fruits

GARDENING IN THE SOUTH

—— with ——
Don Hastings

FLOWERS, VINES, & HOUSEPLANTS

All illustrations property of Taylor Publishing
Company; new illustrations created for this work by
Deborah Jackson-Jones.

Photographs by the author with the exception of a few
graciously supplied by his father.

Designed by Bonnie Baumann

Copyright © 1990 by Donald Hastings, Jr.

Published by Taylor Publishing Company
1550 West Mockingbird Lane
Dallas, Texas 75235

Library of Congress Cataloging in Publication Data

Hastings, Don.
    Flowers, vines & house plants / Don Hastings.
        p.   cm.
    Includes index.
    ISBN 0-87833-600-1
    1. Flower gardening—Southern States.   2. Flowers—Southern
States.   3. Ornamental climbing plants—Southern States.   4. House
plants.   I. Title.   II. Title: Flowers, vines, and houseplants.
III. Series: Hastings, Don. Gardening in the South with Don
Hastings.
SB405.H395   1990
635.9'0975—dc20   90-42084
                                                              CIP

Printed in the United States of America

10 9 8 7 6 5 4 3 2

To
my father,
Donald M. Hastings, Sr.,

horticulturist and superb Southern gardener,

and to
my dearest
Elizabeth Meade Hastings,

wife, editor, and companion

Acknowledgments

In the first two volumes I have listed a number of eminent plantsmen and friends who contributed directly and indirectly to my efforts in writing these books. This third volume is written with full knowledge that many of those listed previously have contributed as much to this volume as to the previous two.

There are a few, however, who have contributed especially to this volume:

Kathy Henderson, my radio and TV partner, whose knowledge and love of perennials is infectious and who chided me more than once when I belittled a plant that she grows and loves.

Donald M. Hastings, Sr., and Tony Roozen, who contributed much to my understanding of bulbs and bulbous-type plants.

Dato Loy Hean Heong, who "kidnapped" me to Malaysia and thus gave me the opportunity to meet many of the plants listed in the house-plant section.

Bernardino Ballesteros and Oscar Opina, who taught me so much about tropical plants.

John Huyck, whom I have acknowledged in Volume II as the best vegetable farmer in the world, who shared the adventure of clearing a jungle and saving Bird's Nest Ferns in the process, as well as being a dear friend and business associate who shares my goal of bringing sophisticated modern agriculture to the remote parts of the world.

George Tee, who would dive into the jungle and proudly identify a potential houseplant.

Don and Chris Hastings, my beloved sons, who have pushed, cajoled, and encouraged me in every step of my writing career. No father could be prouder of his sons than I am.

Elizabeth Meade Hastings, my beloved wife, who read and edited every word in this volume as well as the previous two. I can never express sufficiently my admiration for her ability to make my words sound as they should.

CONTENTS

PLANT NAMES

What is thrift? What is Joseph's Coat? Asking those questions may not seem necessary to you because you are perfectly happy with the name by which you know a certain plant. Unfortunately, a given plant may have several different names depending on the area of the country where you live. Many of you have moved from other parts of the country to the South and find that Southerners call plants that you have grown elsewhere by strange names, even by names known to belong to other plants. Moving from one section of the country to another is difficult enough, but moving from one part of the world to another is even worse. In fact the experts in nomenclature even disagree from time to time.

The three volumes of *Gardening in the South with Don Hastings* had to be written with uniformity of nomenclature, and I had to choose one authority. As far as possible, I have chosen *Hortus Third* by the staff of the Liberty Hyde Bailey Hortorium, Cornell University.

Hortus Third fits our needs well with regard to the plants normally grown in the United States and Canada. However, concerning house plants, there may arise some difficulties. I have found that the local botanical names of many tropical plants are at variance with those listed in *Hortus Third.* Wherever possible and for the sake of uniformity, I have still used the *Hortus Third* name.

In Volume I, I introduced you to the new term 'cultivar' which has replaced the usual term 'variety.' In this series, the only deviation from the use of the term cultivar has been in the part of Volume II dealing with vegetables where the term cultivar is seldom if ever used by seedsmen and seed dealers. I have returned to the use of cultivar in this volume, and you will find this term wherever you might expect to find the term variety.

Another change you might not be accustomed to is the practice of printing the cultivar's name preceded by the abbreviation cv., with the name enclosed in single quotes. Thus the botanical name for Sweet Alyssum will be found as follows: *Lobularia maritima* cv. 'Carpet of Snow,' or perhaps *Lobularia maritima* 'Carpet of Snow.'

I hope that as you move around the country or the world, you will find that this system of identifying plants will help you find the plant you want for your garden or home.

Don Hastings' shaded garden

INTRODUCTION

Gardening in the South with Don Hastings, like my gardening experience, seems to grow and change constantly. It was first conceived as a single comprehensive volume covering all facets of growing plants in the southern United States. Before publication, the editors decided that, rather than cutting the material to make a single thick volume, they would preserve the material in its original state by separating it into three manageable volumes.

When I prepared the original manuscript, I did not know that I would be off once again into strange and wonderful places of the world trying to introduce modern vegetable-growing technology and the concept that private, for-profit agriculture is the answer to the world's food problems.

Volume II, as those who have read it know, was being finalized when I was in the Philippines doing a pilot project which I hoped to expand into a premier vegetable-growing project for that wonderful country. When, unfortunately, it did not work out, I shifted the concept to another Asian country, Malaysia, where governmental and other conditions were highly receptive. The result was a tremendous effort to clear a secondary Malaysian jungle and begin growing world-class vegetables where none had been grown before.

Volume III has grown as a garden grows. Originally it was to be a treatise on flowering plants and vines, but I asked the editors to let me add a chapter on house plants so that I could share the knowledge I have gained from living and working in the tropics, the environment from which so many house plants have come.

Betsy Hastings with a new
Malaysian fruit, Pomelo

Don and Chris Hastings in a large Filipino Mango tree

Working in the jungle is an exciting experience for any plant lover. An infinite variety of extraordinary living things flourish in these forbidding places. One can find the daintiest of flowers, and at the same time monstrous vines, as large as many trees, which choke the life out of everything they wrap around. Animals are just as varied. Huge elephants roamed one area we considered for the farm, while the tiniest deer, the Mouse Deer, ran wild on the land we cultivated.

Rattan Plant

Rattan ready for sale

Allamandas

Bougainvilleas from the Southeast
Orient

Sealing Wax Palm

A Malaysian tea plantation

Producing Rubber Tree

A field of sweet corn growing where there was a jungle eleven months before

Ruby Pielago with a beautiful orchid

Loi Teh Ong with a prize Galia melon grown at American All-Seasons Farms, Paloh Hinai, Malaysia

While the Malaysian jungle experience has enriched the chapter on house plants, the main part of Volume III is about the beautiful flowering plants of the Southern garden. In previous volumes I have written about trees, shrubs, lawns, vegetables, and fruits. Now comes the time to feed the soul with the beauty of flowers.

Flowering plants, especially annuals and perennials, are the ambrosia of the garden. Here are the flowers which for centuries have enriched the lives of civilized people all over the world. In England, these are the plants which constitute the garden. In the South, they have traditionally been "momma's plants," which have made hard times more bearable and which, in today's good times, enrich all of our lives with a beauty found nowhere else.

To me, flowers make a garden. As you know, I love trees, vegetables, and fruits, but flowers have always been a wonderfully special part of our family life. The flower bed outside our country home has brought us great pleasure. It has to be Betsy's garden because Don III, Chris, and I most equate Betsy with its loveliness in our minds. Since she is the human flower of our lives, she naturally becomes the keeper of the loveliest spot we have. She pulls the weeds, loosens the soil, chases the dogs who love to lie in its coolness, and brings in bouquets for our table. When God made flowers with all their soul-feeding beauty, his model must have been a wife and mother such as she.

This volume, like the others, is written for all of us who garden in the South. Though I have written of experiences in other places like Egypt, Kenya, England, the island of Guimaras in the Philippines, and Malaysia, I am always a Southern gardener first, and I see new plants and practices in the light of what I know and want to grow in Sweet Apple. To me, all the wonders of foreign lands come to nothing if they don't add good things to my garden in the place where I belong. Sweet Apple, Georgia, in the southern United States is truly my life and home, and my garden is a wonderful part of that life. Everything I have learned in all the fascinating places I have traveled are soon filed away and forgotten if I cannot add them to what makes my own home garden better.

In Volume III I have tried to provide you with the basics for growing not only garden plants, but also indoor plants. Space limitations prevent me from repeating the details of soil preparation and how to approach growing plants in the southern United States, which are found in Volume I. Likewise, detailed information about starting plants from seed and identifying problems is found in Volume II.

Double Portulaca

Annual Vinca or Periwinkle

CHAPTER 1

FLOWERING PLANTS FOR THE SOUTH

We have made much progress since we started our journey through the Southern garden. The parts of the garden examined so far have been more structural than anything else. We have seen landscaping plants used to form a structure which gives stability and beauty to the home and its surrounding area. Now we come to what I consider the real garden, the area in the landscape where the homeowner displays his or her individuality, love of beauty, and creativity.

The flower garden, which we will visit now, is an area of privacy and intimacy which shows the character and interests of the gardener. Herbaceous flowering plants, as opposed to woody flowering shrubs and trees, are also used in the landscape, but not in the way that they are used in the garden, which we will now examine.

The South has been a sea of green for too long. Now, fortunately, flowering plants are again being creatively used in the landscape by some homeowners and many commercial and residential managers. Throughout the South, commercial and apartment owners have seen the need for masses of flowers in the sea of green. A business or apartment which is well-groomed is not nearly as interesting and appealing as a business or apartment which is

1

A planting of petunias at the entrance to an office park

well-groomed *and* planted with colorful flowers. The owners of these properties should be congratulated because these people show they care about the community at large by providing beauty for the passer-by.

ESTABLISHING THE FLOWER GARDEN

The intimate use of flowers in our individual lives and within our gardens, however, is something quite different from the use of masses of flowers in commercial areas or even in sweeps in our landscape.

I like to think of trees and shrubs as the Paul Bunyans of the landscape. They are the adults, the strength and stability. To me, flowers are like beautiful children, happy and fun to be with. They are little girls dressed for Easter and little boys full of activity. Flowers in the private garden should be lively, interesting, and ever-changing. They can also be bearers of peace and serenity.

A flower bed can be bright and colorful all summer and fall.

I shall always remember the postage stamp gardens behind the attached houses in the industrial parts of London. Amidst the surrounding grime are these little areas of beauty which have tremendous meaning for the gardeners who created them. These blue-collar workers cultivate four features to remain sane in an insane world: the family, the dog, the nearby pub, and the garden.

The garden as an intimate personal retreat does not exist for most people. Too many are involved in such a whirligig of activity that they have neither the time required to create such a spot, nor the time to sit and be tranquilized by what they have created. What a pity, for we search for entertainment away from our homes and fail to take advantage of the extraordinary potential in our own back yards.

That potential for a garden retreat is there waiting for us to develop. Let's make a pact with each other that we will try. I was told by a landscape architect that people don't want a place for flowers because growing them is too much trouble. I can't believe that. I think we have just forgotten how to use them. Let's find out how easy it really is.

CHOOSING THE LOCATION

A flower garden can be almost anywhere on the property, but the nearer the living area the better. It may be in the sun, the shade, or anywhere between, because there are flowers which will grow in the open and flowers which will grow in the shadows or shade of the house or trees.

Place flower beds where they may be enjoyed constantly.

Groups of a few plants are easily maintained.

3

I always admonish the new flower gardener to start with a small area. Learn how much time a small area takes and expand if you find you have more time than that. It is better to have a beautiful small garden that requires only the time you wish to spend than a large area which makes gardening a real chore. I have a 20-acre piece of property, yet my flower garden is only four feet wide and twenty feet long. Despite its relatively small size in the total scheme of our property, it is one of the most meaningful areas we have.

Place the garden where you will enjoy it most. When planning the landscape design, you, or you and your landscape designer or architect, should determine where you want your flower and herbaceous plant beds. In planning the garden location, you are planning the location of a living area which is just as important as where the garage or porch will be. The main consideration is to locate a flower garden where you, your family, and your friends will enjoy it.

The area may be around a patio or adjacent to a deck. The walk area may be grass, bricks, stones, or flagstone. The design of the beds should be pleasing and intimate. Privacy is created with structures like fences and walls or with background shrubs. Plan these to complement the flowering plants you will be growing. Think of the area as your own private paradise where you enjoy working and relaxing.

There are two ways to approach locating the flower garden:
- Choose an area that fits into your landscape design or outdoor living plans and select the best plants for those conditions; or
- Choose an area that is suited for the types of flowering plants you enjoy and have decided that you would like to grow.

In the first instance you choose plants to fit a spot, and in the second you choose a spot to fit the types of plants you will be growing. Perhaps the ideal spot for your flower garden is shady. You must then choose shade-loving plants for those you will grow. However, if you decide that you wish to grow marigolds and Salvia, you must find a suitable sunny location.

Choose the right types of plants for a shady spot.

LIGHT EXPOSURE

The light exposure your flower bed receives is of great importance in determining what you can grow. Sun, part sun, moderate shade, and full shade are possible exposures, and a variety of plants will grow in each of these areas. However, sun-loving plants will do poorly in the shade and shade plants will not do well, or perhaps even die, in too much sun. Exposure is essential in choosing your flower area.

Ideally, flower areas should combine various exposures to allow a broader use of plant material. My own flower bed was placed to encompass a wide range of exposure from deep shade to bright sun. I chose an area which could be viewed from our house. I started the bed under two trees and then extended it outward into the open back yard. With this arrangement I am able to grow all types of plants and have the enjoyment of many contrasts in flowers and foliage.

Measure the amount of sun or shade which your area has. Light is as important as direct sun. Gardens under high canopies of tree limbs may take moderate-shade plants; gardens under low limbs can take only full-shade plants.

Sun-loving plants should have at least six hours of full, uninterrupted sun each day. Cool weather plants, especially perennials, do best if they have morning sun rather than afternoon sun. However, hot weather plants can generally take either morning or afternoon sun.

PREPARING THE FLOWER BED

Flowers need good soil, good drainage, and generally everything which trees, shrubs, roses, lawns, vegetables, and fruits need. Since these things have been covered in previous volumes of *Gardening in the South*, the only thing I would add here is that you should prepare your flower beds even better than the vegetable garden, where large numbers of plants are also grown in a small amount of space. Just as with vegetables, good drainage is of major importance because few herbaceous plants will grow well in

After adding all the right ingredients the bed needs a thorough soaking before planting.

5

poorly-drained soil. Good drainage is of particular importance with bulbs, for most bulbs develop poorly in tight, sticky, badly-drained soil.

The pH range of most flower beds should be about 6.0 to 6.5. This is high for many of our broadleaf evergreens, especially Azaleas and Camellias, and you may need to sacrifice some flowering plant vigor to keep from damaging background shrubs. Never add lime to flower beds which are near acid-loving plants.

Dig or till the bed deeply; work in liberal amounts of finely-ground bark and peat moss, and add dehydrated cattle manure or an organic material like OST. If the area has poor drainage, add liberal amounts of perlite to loosen the soil and let excess water move through and away from the roots of the plants.

A good formula for a 100-square-foot bed area in heavy clay soil is:
- One bag of finely-ground bark
- One six-cubic-foot bale of peat moss
- One three-cubic-foot bag of perlite
- Twenty-five pounds of dehydrated cattle manure or OST
- Ten pounds of a 5-10-15 fertilizer at planting time
- If lime is needed, add 10 pounds of dolomitic limestone.

I till my area once and then begin to work in each of these ingredients. The ground bark and peat moss may be worked in together. Then work in the perlite, cattle manure, and/or OST. Rake the bed once, spread the correct amounts of 5-10-15 and limestone, and rake again until they are integrated into the top three to four inches of the soil.

The secret to success in a flower bed is to have an extremely loose and porous texture which is free from rocks, clods, old plant material, weeds, and debris of any kind. When I finish preparing my flower bed I can plant easily using only my hands without the use of a trowel.

CHOOSING WHAT TO PLANT

We will examine the plants for this garden in groups. Though you may not use the groups separately, I will discuss them in this manner for ease in determining how to plant and grow them.

Salvia and Vinca are good examples of annuals for Southern gardens.

Hosta is a hardy perennial.

Cleome is an annual which reseeds so freely that replanting is not necessary for a new season of bloom.

King Alfred daffodils will remain in the garden for many years.

Geraniums are perennials which can be used as annuals.

- **Annuals:** These are herbaceous plants which grow from a seed to a mature plant and then die, all in one season.
- **Biennials:** These are herbaceous plants which grow, mature, and die in two seasons, usually having vegetative growth the first season and flowers the second.
- **Perennials:** These are herbaceous plants which last for over three seasons, often for many years.
- **Bulb and bulbous-type plants:** Though this is not a botanically-correct classification, I use it to help your planning. These are perennials which grow back from an underground storage organ.

There are other minor divisions of this group of plants which it will be helpful to understand:

- **Perennials which act as annuals:** These are plants like Impatiens (Sultana) which grow, bloom, and die in one season in the mid-South, but grow for many years in areas where there is no frost.
- **Reseeding plants, usually annuals:** These plants drop many viable seeds on the ground underneath and each year will come back from these new plants, making the colony seem perennial. A good example is Cleome (Spider Plant).

Catalogues and other garden publications use a number of abbreviations to identify plants.

- **T (Tender):** This indicates that a plant will not survive freezing temperatures. It is used with annual and perennial designations, TA and TP.
- **HA (Hardy Annual):** This indicates that a plant can withstand light freezing temperatures but still completes its cycle in one year. It is important because these plants may be set out earlier in the spring than others.
- **HHA (Half-Hardy Annual):** These are annuals which can withstand frost but not freezing temperatures.
- **HP (Hardy Perennial):** These are perennials which can withstand frost or freezing and will last for many years.

STARTING FROM SEEDS OR PLANTS

The question of whether to buy plants or grow your own plants from seed is often bothersome. Starting your annuals, biennials, and perennials from seed means planning ahead. If you wait until the impetus of beautiful spring weather inspires you into starting a garden, you may be too late to enjoy the full potential of your plantings.

The biggest advantage of starting your own seedlings is that you will have a much wider choice from seed catalogs, which list hundreds of different types and cultivars, than you will have in most plant stores and nurseries, which have the space to carry only a few cultivars of each type.

Starting seeds inside before the season

After the seeds have germinated and developed a strong plant, remove the plastic bag.

8

Buying ahead from seed catalogs allows better choices of colors, heights, and forms of a given type of plant.

Growing your own seedlings is an inexpensive way to get the best, and it is fun. You must do it right, however, to be successful. In Volume II, you will find a section on growing plants from seed. The emphasis was on vegetables but the principles are exactly the same.

When you buy plants from a plant store or seed outlet, observe the following rules:

- Purchase plants grown in cells or individual pots. These may be removed easily and planted without danger of breaking the roots. Plants grown together in a tray must be pulled apart, often causing damage to the stem or roots.
- Buy fresh plants. Find out which day new shipments are due to arrive and plan to be at the plant shop or nursery. Choices will be better and the plants will transplant and grow off better.
- Purchase plants at the beginning of the planting season. Choices are far better and the plants will always be fresher and more vigorous.
- Purchase plants on the day they are to be planted. It is difficult for you to provide for these seedlings as well as the nursery. Allowing them to wilt or to stay too long in the pot or cell pack may be harmful and prevent rapid development once they are planted.
- Always check the roots of one of the plants in a cell tray or in a pot. The roots should be white and healthy looking. Do not buy plants with brown, heavily-bound roots.

Biennials and perennials may also be purchased as dormant roots during the late fall and winter. This is an ideal way to start them since dormant roots are generally less expensive than plants growing in pots and are easier to handle without damaging.

If you use dormant roots, you can start your plants earlier and let them develop with the spring. First-year growth should be greater and performance better.

Buy your plants growing in cell packs or individual pots.

There are some drawbacks to using dormant roots. The main one is that you must plan ahead. Also, beds must be worked earlier and space left for annuals which cannot be planted until later.

PLANTING YOUR FLOWER GARDEN

Take your plants home and plant them immediately. Leave the plants in the cell pack or in the pot until you are ready to put them in the ground. I mark where each group of plants will go; then I dig the holes, remove the plants from the cells or pots and squeeze the ball in the palm of my hand to loosen the roots. Plant each one slightly deeper than it was growing in the cell or pot. Press the soil tightly around the ball of earth. When all have been planted, water the bed thoroughly using a hose with a water breaker. Be sure the soil is thoroughly settled around the roots of the new seedlings and that there are no air pockets next to the roots.

Planting dormant roots is also easy. Purchase the plants when the bed is ready and plant them immediately. They may be dormant, but they should neither dry out nor be too wet. If you cannot plant them immediately, keep them in the package in a place which is cool but will not freeze.

When ready to plant, make a plant marker for each group of the same type or make an accurate planting chart. Remember, these plants may not sprout for some time and you will want to know exactly where they are, especially if you will be adding annuals or bulbs to the same area.

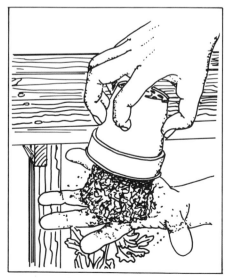

Carefully remove the plant from its pot. If grown in a peat pot, be sure to remove the pressed peat.

Squeeze the ball of soil and loosen the roots with your fingers by carefully pulling them away from the ball of soil.

KEEPING FLOWERING PLANTS GROWING AND BLOOMING

Flowering plants are subject to many of the same nutrient requirements, watering needs, insects, diseases, and growth problems associated with other types of plants, especially vegetables.

Fertilizing Your Flower Bed

Herbaceous plants grow rapidly and thus have a high demand for fertilizer. The initial application when the bed was prepared will last for only about six weeks. Additional amounts of the 5-10-15 fertilizer should be given to insure continued growth and bloom. Usually, an application after six weeks should be followed by another one in the late summer. However, if the growth rate is low and the weather is hot and dry, reduce the application rate by one-half.

Watering Your Flower Garden

Most of our flowers are planted so that much of the early growth comes during our best growing weather. The South's wonderful spring, however, may be followed by hot, dry weather. At this time your plants may need help. Follow these rules which I have set forth over and over:

- Water **thoroughly** each time you water; never sprinkle lightly.
- Apply at least one-half inch of water per watering.
- Water again in three or four days if no rain occurs.
- Use a water breaker on your hose if watering by hand or use a fine sprinkler to prevent beating down small plants.
- Water in the morning if you will be wetting the foliage. This allows the plants to dry before the cool, still evening, reducing insect and disease potential.
- Whenever possible, soak the bed rather than top-watering.

Insects and Diseases

Beautiful herbaceous plants grow rapidly and succulently, which is a delight to many insects and diseases. Spider mites, thrips, leaf hoppers,

Water breaker

worms of all sorts, slugs, and snails are but a few of the many insects which may cause problems. Mildew is one of the worst of our disease problems with many plants, especially Zinnias and some forms of Phlox.

In the section "Being A Good Detective" found in Volume II, I have described how to identify the various problems you may encounter.

Growth Problems

The purpose of a flower garden is to have plants which create beauty and enhance the environment around the home. Poorly growing plants are not attractive and detract from the environment. Growth problems are usually the result of poor soil preparation, planting the wrong plant in a given spot, inadequate nutrients from fertilizing programs, and bad watering practices. Follow the rules for fertilizing, watering, and disease control, and learn to spot the symptoms of the various growth problems. Then react quickly so that your plants may recover and perform as you want them to.

Grooming Your Plants

Herbaceous flowering plants must grow rapidly to bloom as well as expected. However, continued flowering can be encouraged by removing the old spent flowers from the plant, thereby removing the seed development parts that take precedence over vegetative growth and flower bud initiation. Besides, plants look much better when they are putting on new flowers and not keeping old ones.

Some plants, like annual Hollyhock and Snapdragons, begin to play out toward the end of the summer. Cut them back rather severely, fertilize them, and water if it is dry. As the nights get cooler, they may put on a new burst of growth, followed by a very good bloom.

Staking and Tying

Many herbaceous plants may get rather tall and begin to topple over when it rains. I stake most of my tall growing plants with simple, inexpensive small green bamboo stakes and tie them with green jute twine. Dahlias and other very tall plants may require a longer, heavier bamboo stake or a steel plant prop.

Several types of flowers give tremendous interest to a garden.

ALL ABOUT ANNUALS FOR THE SOUTH

Annuals make up the bulk of the flower plantings in our gardens. They are generally easier to grow than perennials and quickly perform to our expectations. The new gardener should concentrate upon the tremendous range of annuals which are suitable for the South. Add to them permanent plants (perennials) which are proven to require low maintenance. Having a perennial plant that will "come back" each year is sometimes overwhelmingly appealing, and many gardeners plant perennials with little thought of the effort required to keep them growing well.

In choosing annuals I like using different textures, colors, bloom forms, and heights. I never have great masses of any single type but plan the garden bed with small groups of the same kind of plants, in ever-changing blocks of color.

Don't let anyone dictate what you will plant. Groups that please you may be unacceptable to others, but remember this is your private place, and what you enjoy is what you should plant within the constraints of the requirements of the plants themselves. Kathy Henderson, my partner in radio and television, has enriched my knowledge and appreciation when it comes to herbaceous plants. Kathy exudes to all who know her not only great knowledge of these plants, but also a real love for each as an individual, rather than a great mass of color or form or texture. I have seen her dive into a mass of weeds and show me a beautiful flower with the same feeling for its individuality and worth as if we were meeting a fine person in a crowd of ordinary people. Kathy loves plants as plants and I hope you will learn to also.

Therefore, I will not tell you what to grow in your flower garden. It is your personal choice. Seed catalogues, especially the really well-prepared ones, will show a wide range from which to choose. Seedsmen are doing a marvelous job introducing new varieties and types of flowers for the garden. The All-American Seed Selection group judges many new introductions each year and chooses the most outstanding for their annual awards. The European seedsmen have similar judgings, and they award prizes for their best. Not all of these nationally and internationally acclaimed introductions will perform better in the South than our old favorites. My practice is to never depend entirely upon something new to replace an old well-tried and proven plant. However, don't be afraid of trying some new cultivar. Plant a few and see if it is better than the one you have been growing.

My list of possible flowering and foliage plants for the South contains over 100 names. That's far too many for a book like this and must be reserved for a book on these plants alone. So don't be upset if your favorite or one which you have seen is omitted. I hope you will try many more than the few which I write about here. Remember, you are dealing with plants that are not necessary for the landscape, and losing one is not like losing a beautiful oak or even a wonderful flowering shrub. If Snapdragons are a failure for you, so be it. Next year plant something else or even drop in a known performer when you see the snaps looking ratty.

The following is a list of plants which are friends of mine. Among them you will find flowering plants as well as colorful foliage plants. Don't be afraid to experiment. I grow many peppers, ornamental and useful, in my flower bed. These unusual plants offer something interesting and add a great deal to my garden.

All the plants I am listing have been happy and done well in my garden. Maybe you will adopt them as your friends also, but if you have other friends that is fine. Garden plants are too personal for anyone to say that his plants are the best.

AGERATUM
Ageratum Houstonianum

Class: TA
Height Range: Low
Colors: Blue, pink, royal purple, and white
Exposure: Sun to part shade
Best Cultivars: Compact ones like 'Blue Surf' and 'Blue Mink'
How to Start: From seed sown inside early
When to Transplant: After frost
Use: Beds or borders

The Ageratums are easy to grow but should have good drainage and rich soil. They will last all summer. I like the blues best because the whites look dirty and the pinks are not as colorful. The old-fashioned Ageratum grows tall and reseeds readily, sometimes becoming a pest; avoid it because it is loose and stalky. Reseeded cultivars revert to this form and need to be removed.

Ageratum may be subject to attacks of spider mites. Watch for mottling of the leaves and spray with Kelthane or Orthene when they are a problem.

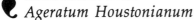

ALTERNANTHERA or JOSEPH'S COAT
Alternanthera ficoidea

Class: TP, used as an annual
Height Range: Medium when pruned correctly
Colors: Red, yellow, and green leaves
Exposure: Sun for best leaf variegation
Best Cultivars: 'Bettzickiana'
How to Start: Cuttings from mother plants
When to Transplant: When warm, after frost
Use: Edging

I don't see as much Alternanthera as I once did and I miss it. The brightly-colored foliage covers the compact plant. Prune it like a small shrub to keep it at the desired height and to force fresh colorful growth all along.

Take cuttings in the fall and pot off the young plants to overwinter and have stock plants for more cuttings in the spring.

Alternanthera is a trouble-free plant which performs best during the hot weather of Southern summers. Do not overwater or force growth because when it is in heavy growth, its color is not as bright.

SWEET ALYSSUM
Lobularia maritima

Class: TA
Height Range: Low
Colors: White, pink, rose, and purple
Exposure: Sun
Best Cultivars: 'Royal Carpet,' purple, and 'Carpet of Snow,' white
How to Start: Sow inside or sow where they will be growing, and then thin to 6 inches apart
When to Transplant: Seed in early April or transplant after frost
Use: Edging and borders

The Sweet Alyssum is a dainty carpet-like plant which provides a mass of fragrant blossoms. Heavy rain may beat them down, but they will straighten up again. Grow them in areas which are rich and well-drained for they do poorly in tight, sticky soil.

Do not overwater Alyssum. Root rot and fungus problems may ruin your plants.

JOSEPH'S COAT AMARANTHUS AND SUMMER POINSETTIA
Amaranthus tricolor and *A. tricolor* cv. 'Splendens'

Class: TA
Height Range: Tall
Colors: Red, green, and gold, or only red

Exposure: Full sun
Best Cultivars: 'Illumination,' red-topped gold, and 'Joseph's Coat,' red, green, and gold variegated
How to Start: Inside and transplant
When to Transplant: After weather warms
Use: Tall accent or discussion plant

These tall, rather gross plants are highly prized by many. The *A. tricolor* has green, yellow, and red variegated leaves, and the *A. tricolor splendens* has huge fountains of red leaves. They are too big for most gardens but are unique where there is room. If you overplant with too many, it takes away from the interest.

Amaranthus love hot weather and are ideal for late summer color when so many cool weather annuals begin to play out.

BALSAM or TOUCH-ME-NOT
Impatiens Balsamea

Class: TA
Height Range: Medium
Colors: Pale pink, red, and white
Exposure: Sun to part shade
Best Cultivars: Camellia-flowered types
How to Start: Start seed inside
When to Transplant: After frost
Use: Beds

The Balsam blooms through the entire summer and gives good color when many other flowers are suffering from heat. It is kin to the Sultana but will take more sun. Since it tends to be a bit stiff and since the New Guinea Hybrid Sultanas may be grown in the sun, I seldom plant Balsam anymore. It will reseed in a bed and may come back the second year in droves.

BASIL
Ocimum Basilicum

Class: TA
Height Range: Medium
Colors: Green or purple-leaf types
Exposure: Sun
Best Cultivars: 'Dark Opal' or regular green specie
How to Start: Seed inside
When to Transplant: After frost
Use: Ornamental use as well as for aromatic leaves

I prefer 'Dark Opal' Basil to the green because it is so colorful in the garden. The leaves are not as aromatic as the green form but are still useable in the kitchen. It makes an interesting plant and is a bright addition when grown in contrast to yellow marigolds. Be sure to give it good drainage.

A mass of blue Ageratum in front of pink Begonias

Dark Opal Basil

Dwarf Ageratum

Royal Carpet Alyssum

Summer poinsettia, Amaranthus Molten Fire

🌱 WAX BEGONIA
Begonia X *semperflorens–cultorum*

Class: TA
Height Range: Low to medium
Colors: Red, pink, white, and multicolored; leaves may be green, copper, or deep red
Exposure: Sun to moderate shade, depending on cultivar
Best Cultivars: Many; choose for the leaf and flower colors
How to Start: Cuttings or buy plants; seeds are tiny
When to Transplant: After frost
Use: Borders, edges, mass plantings, and for spots of color

The Wax Begonias are some of our best flowering plants in the summer garden. They have few problems except that they don't grow well in poorly-drained soil. They will take some shade; in too-deep shade they will tend to be leggy and have fewer blossoms. Too-hot sun is also bad for some cultivars.

I make cuttings every fall and carry over stock plants to chop up into more cuttings the following spring. They will live inside, and sometimes bloom, if you have a warm sunny spot.

There are many other types of Begonias which may be used in the garden, including the beautiful Angel Wing types. They all root easily. You can make cuttings in the fall before frost for plants to overwinter. Start new fresh plants from these stock plants to have plenty for the flower bed.

Begonias are beautiful as individual plants or in masses of color. They do as well in planter boxes and large pots as in garden soil. Do not overlook the hanging basket Begonias with long stems which will weep away from the basket. Although they do not have the interesting blossoms of the Wax Begonias, they are definitely worthwhile.

I think you will find the whole Begonia group to be one of your favorites.

🌱 BROWALLIA
Browallia sp.

Class: TA
Height Range: Medium
Colors: Blue and white
Exposure: Sun to moderate shade
Best Cultivars: Low (10 inches): 'Blue Troll' and 'White Troll;' Medium (14–18 inches): 'Blue Bells' and 'Silver Bells'
How to Start: Seed
When to Transplant: After frost
Use: Beds or pots, even hanging baskets

Browallia is a little-used but excellent annual for shady places and for pots, planters, and tubs. It flowers constantly during the summer. Potted plants may also be brought inside for winter bloom. Start fresh plants for the next year, however, because the plants get stemmy when used a second year.

White wax leaf Begonias

Wax leaf Begonias

Wax leaf Begonias

Browallia

BURNING BUSH
Kochia scoparia cv. 'Childsii'

Class: TA
Height Range: Tall
Colors: A cypress-like foliage which turns brilliant red in late summer and fall
Exposure: Sun
Best Cultivars: Cultivar 'Childsii' is the best to grow
How to Start: Sow seed in beds or start them inside
When to Transplant: After frost
Use: Individual specimens or as background annual hedge, or may be grown in tubs

Burning Bush is an unusual old favorite, ideal as a quick background plant for other annuals. In the fall it looks as if it is on fire.

ORNAMENTAL CABBAGE AND KALE
Brassica oleracea, Acephala Group

Class: HHA
Height Range: Medium to tall
Colors: Yellow and royal purple on green
Exposure: Sun
Best Cultivars: Various, according to color desired
How to Start: Seed inside
When to Transplant: After hard freezes
Use: Beds

I list the Flowering Cabbage and Kale not because I like them but because they are grown so widely. Frankly, I think they are gross-looking but apparently others do not.

Use them sparingly rather than in great masses in large beds. Whereas one or two are interesting, more look like a diseased cabbage patch.

They also make good pot plants. Set them out very early, about the time you set cabbage in the garden. They last through the summer. If loopers attack, control them with Dipel. Their best show is in the fall when it is cool, and they will last until hard freezes occur.

CALENDULA
Calendula officinalis

Class: HHA
Height Range: Medium
Colors: Yellow, orange
Exposure: Sun to light shade
Best Cultivars: 'Golden Gem,' 'Fiesta Gitana,' 'Yellow Gitana'

Ornamental Kale

Kochia, Burning Bush

Calendula

Celosia, feather type

Cleome

How to Start: Start early inside, or sow as ground warms
When to Transplant: After hard freezes have passed
Use: Beds, planters, or pots

Calendulas are excellent flowers for the early spring or fall, but they do poorly when it is hot. Generally it is wise to grow two crops, one in the spring and one for fall. They will withstand light frost and bloom until freezing weather in the fall.

CELOSIA: FEATHERS AND COCKSCOMBS
Celosia argentea

Class: TA
Height Range: Medium to tall
Colors: Red, yellow, orange
Exposure: Sun
Best Cultivars: Feathers, *C. a. plumosa:* 'Golden Triumph,' gold; Crested, *C. a. cristata:* 'Toreador,' red
How to Start: Seed inside or sow directly in good soil
When to Transplant: After frost
Use: Beds or groups of a few plants

The Cockscombs and Feathers are brilliant and most unusual plants for a unique effect. Because they have a strong appearance, they are not suited to every flower bed, but when properly used they can add a great deal. The plumes of the feathers are long and borne on tall plants, while the crested types are more low-growing and quite unusual, the heads resembling the comb of a rooster. They need good soil, hot weather, and full sun to do well.

CLEOME or SPIDER PLANT
Cleome Hasslerana

Class: TA
Height Range: Tall
Colors: Pink, white, rose, and lavender
Exposure: Sun to very light shade
Best Cultivars: The 'Queen' series
How to Start: Seed inside or sow after ground warms
When to Transplant: After frost
Use: Tall background plants

Here is a virtually trouble-free plant which not only is easily seeded directly into good garden soil, but also can be started inside in pots ahead of setting time. The light and airy flowers form freely on the plant. Once established, they reseed freely and come back each year with no problems. The only real difficulty is that they reseed too freely and may become a pest.

COLEUS
Coleus X hibridus

Class: TP
Height Range: Low to medium
Colors: Many variegations of yellow, pink, and red
Exposure: Sun to moderate shade
Best Cultivars: Many from which to choose
How to Start: Cuttings or from seed started inside
When to Transplant: After frost
Use: Beds, borders, pots, tubs, and planters

The common garden Coleus is one of our most satisfactory plants for shade. The brightly-colored leaves add a great deal to any planting and will enliven otherwise dreary areas in the shade. Some of the newer cultivars will also take sun.

Coleus needs good soil and drainage, for it does poorly in soggy soil. If you give it fertilizer during the growing season and keep the flower heads pinched off, you will have a trouble-free plant. If you see mealybugs, leafhoppers, or aphids, just spray with Malathion or a good general insecticide.

I like to take cuttings from the best leaf forms and colors just before frost. After these are rooted, I pot them for winter color and grow them in a sunny window. In the late winter, I make a number of cuttings from these mother plants for the new spring crops to set back in the flower border after frost has passed.

DWARF DAHLIA
Dahlia X

Class: P, grown as an annual
Height Range: Medium as an annual
Colors: Usually mixtures of yellow, red, lavender, pink, orange, white
Exposure: Sun
Best Cultivars: 'Redskin,' 'Elite,' 'Rigoletto'
How to Start: Start seed inside
When to Transplant: After ground warms and after frost
Use: Beds and groups

I use Dwarf Dahlias every year in my little flower bed because they give me more joy than any other plant. They are stocky, though they need staking by August, and they produce flowers for enjoyment in the garden and for cutting.

The most stocky and manageable plants come from seed each year, though I try to save a few favorite colors by lifting and storing the tubers. These plants never are as satisfactory as the new seedlings because they always grow taller and flop over, necessitating early staking, which most of the time I forget to do.

Dwarf Dahlias are really easy to start from seed since the seeds are large and germinate rather quickly. They are tough and easy to pot off. I grow them into nice plants to set in the garden after frost.

Dwarf Dahlia grown from seed

Dwarf Dahlias bloom the first summer

Single Gloriosa Daisy

Double Gloriosa Daisy

Coleus

ENGLISH DAISY
Bellis perennis

Class: P, used as a cool-season annual
Height Range: Very low
Colors: White, pink, rose
Exposure: Sun to moderate shade
Best Cultivars: Mixed specie
How to Start: Start in seed trays in September
When to Transplant: As weather cools in the fall
Use: Winter beds or border plants, often with Pansies

The English Daisy is a plant we should grow for winter flowers in the South. They seldom survive our summers; if they do, they grow ratty-looking. The idea is to plant them in the garden in October and have a good fall bloom and additional flowers whenever the weather is mild in the winter. In the spring they really burst forth once again. Most gardeners use them along with Pansies, which they treat in the same way. Start the seed in a seed tray in early September, pot as soon as large enough to handle, and set out when the plants are stocky.

Pull them up when the weather gets hot and they stop flowering.

GLORIOSA DAISY
Rudbeckia hirta cv. 'Gloriosa Daisy'

Class: HP, but often used as an annual
Height Range: Medium to tall
Colors: Orange with dark center
Exposure: Sun to light shade
Best Cultivars: Single and double
How to Start: Seed inside or sow directly in beds
When to Transplant: As soon as soil can be worked
Use: Tall massed plantings or groups in a bed

The Gloriosa Daisy is an easy-to-grow perennial which I list here because many gardeners use it as an annual. Start plants inside early and set the young plants in the garden after hard freezes have passed. They will be blooming profusely by June and give summer color in abundance. The trouble-free Gloriosa Daisy will last for years if you wish. However, I usually plant new ones yearly and move them around the flower bed so that there is some change each summer.

The doubles are not as pretty as the huge singles, in my opinion, but you may think differently. Either one is a plant which you should have in your garden.

DIANTHUS or GARDEN PINKS
Dianthus sp., mainly *Dianthus chinensis*

Class: HHA
Height Range: 8 to 12 inches

Colors: Reds, whites, pinks, and mixes
Exposure: Full sun
Best Cultivars: There are a number of cultivars which have proved very satis-
factory. The following should be considered: 'Telstar,' mixed 'Fire Carpet,'
bright red 'Double Gaity,' mixed
How to Start: Start inside in seed flats
When to Transplant: After frost danger
Use: Bedding and borders

The annual Garden Pinks do well when planted in full sun and in exceptionally well-drained soil. Masses of these beautiful plants when covered with their
spicy fragrant flowers give an outstanding addition to the flower garden.

❦ DUSTY MILLER
Senecio Cineraria

Class: HHP used as an annual
Height Range: Low to medium
Colors: Silver-gray leaves
Exposure: Sun
Best Cultivars: Choose according to the texture and height desired
How to Start: Start seed inside in the winter
When to Transplant: After frost
Use: Beds and borders

The Dusty Millers are Mediterranean-region natives which will take hot sun
and poor soil, provided they drain well. They are used for their unusual fuzzy and
silver-gray leaves. They make wonderful borders to contrast with rich green
shrubs.

Everybody has gone nuts over the finely lace-leafed cultivars, but I prefer the
more solid leaf forms. They make a much better contrast with Salvia and other
heavy-leafed annuals.

It is better to use the Dusty Millers as annuals even though they may overwinter when the Arctic Expresses leave us alone. They tend to become woody
with time and it is best to have the fresh young plants.

Start seed well ahead of setting time because it will be a while before the
seedlings are tough enough to set out. Plant in the open after frost.

❦ FOXGLOVE
Digitalis purpurea

Class: HB
Height Range: Tall, sometimes very tall
Colors: White, purple, pink, lavender, yellow
Exposure: Sun to part shade
Best Cultivars: 'Foxy' (quick blooming), 'Excelsior'
How to Start: Start seed indoors very early

Large-leaved Dusty Miller

Fine-leaved Dusty Miller

Trailing geranium, Philippines

Foxgloves, reseeding biennial

Garden geranium

27

When to Transplant: As soon as weather warms
Use: Striking background or groups

The Foxgloves are most satisfactory if you will give them a partly sunny place and plenty of rich, well-drained soil. They will bloom the first year if started early and set while the weather is cool. They may also be started in the early fall and set out as the ground cools. They will bloom earlier when set in the fall. 'Foxy' is smaller-growing and blooms more quickly.

Plant Foxgloves in an area which is left undisturbed; they will reseed themselves and you will always have plants to bloom.

GARDEN GERANIUM
Pelargonium X hortorum

Class: TP
Height Range: Medium to tall
Colors: White, red, pink, salmon, coral
Exposure: Sun
Best Cultivars: 'Red Elite,' 'Sprinter' series, 'Orbit' series
How to Start: Seed or cuttings
When to Transplant: After frost when the weather is warming
Use: Beds, pots, planters, tubs

Though Garden Geraniums are always a favorite, you may have trouble keeping them in heavy bloom when you mix them with other plants with different requirements. Thus it is best to have them in blocks of color so you can temper properly the area in which they are growing.

They prefer a well-drained and not too rich soil with a pH about 6.5. Over-fertilizing causes excessive growth and poor blossoming. Poor drainage and too acid soil will result in very poor, scrawny growth. In pots they like to be pot-bound, and should not be shifted into larger pots until they begin to show growth problems.

Geraniums do best in morning and noonday sun with a little shade from the hot afternoon sun. They need a high phosphate and potash fertilizer like a 5-10-15. Do not overwater; they do best on the dry side.

Remove all the old, spent blossoms from Geraniums so that they will continue to blossom through the season. Make cuttings in the fall and have pot plants for sunny windows in winter. Then make cuttings from these plants to have plenty for the garden next spring.

You may also take up Geraniums, top, roots, and all, and store them for the winter. I dig my Geraniums and shake the excess dirt off the roots, then lay them on a piece of newspaper in the garage to dry down. When they are dry, I shake off the loose dry soil, lay them on a newspaper, and fold the bottom of the paper over the roots, leaving the tops exposed. Store them this way in a cool place where they will not freeze. In the spring, cut the plants back, pot them, or simply plant in the garden when it is warm. Not all of your plants will survive this storage but even the few which come through will be worth the effort.

There are many Geraniums which are not often used. I particularly like some of the new hanging basket types and the scented foliage types.

GOMPHRENA or GLOBE AMARANTH
Gomphrena globosa

Class: TA
Height Range: Low to medium
Colors: Purple, red, white
Exposure: Sun to light shade
Best Cultivars: 'Buddy,' very compact and low growing; Tall Mixed Gomphrena has a range of colors
How to Start: From seed, inside
When to Transplant: After frost
Use: Beds or borders (flowers may be dried)

The Globe Amaranth is an excellent hot-weather annual for sunny borders or light shade. The dwarf compact forms are best since the tall ones tend to grow floppy. Their only other requirement is that they cannot be grown in sticky soil.

HELIOTROPE
Heliotropium arborescens

Class: TP, used as a summer annual
Height Range: Medium to tall
Colors: Rich purple
Exposure: Sun to light shade
Best Cultivars: The specie and 'Marine'
How to Start: Start seed inside
When to Transplant: After weather warms
Use: Tall bedding plants

Heliotrope is a plant which really connotes an English garden. It has huge purple heads of mildly fragrant flowers on strong, tall plants. Growing them adjacent to the pale pink Silver Puff Hollyhock makes a beautiful color combination, and my plantings always bring about much discussion for it is a seldom-used plant.

Plant when there is no chance of cold nights since cold makes them stunt and develop poorly.

HOLLYHOCK
Alcea rosea

Class: A, Hardy Biennial
Height Range: Medium to tall
Colors: White, pink, rose, red, yellow
Exposure: Sun
Best Cultivars: 'Silver Puff,' 'Summer Carnival,' 'Majorette'
How to Start: Start seed inside
When to Transplant: After frost
Use: Bedding in groups, with tall biennials planted in the background

Silver Puff hollyhock used as
an annual

White Impatiens and blue Ageratum

Coral and red Impatiens

Biennial hollyhock

New Guinea hybrid Impatiens

Bed of New Guinea hybrid Impatiens

The Hollyhock of old with its tall, leggy form has been replaced by the so-called annual Hollyhocks which will blossom the first year from seed and which should be replanted each year. They are also more bushy, and most importantly, they are resistant to the rust disease which attacks the biennial types so badly.

Plant them in rich soil which, guess what, should be well-drained! I repeat that over and over but it *is* so important.

I have always been partial to 'Silver Puff' because it is still the prettiest, but it is hard to find these days. Other widely-grown annuals are 'Summer Carnival' (tall) and 'Majorette' (medium). These latter two come mixed, which I don't really like when I am planning colors. However, they are worthwhile for their spectacular blossoms.

Remove the old flowers and seed pods of Hollyhocks and groom them back every now and then to keep them growing and flowering well.

🌱 IMPATIENS or SULTANA
Impatiens Wallerana

Class: TP, used as an annual in the garden
Height Range: Low to medium
Colors: White, orange, coral, salmon, red, pink, purple, and variegations of the strong colors with white
Exposure: Light to moderate shade, heavier shade in rich loose soil which is well-drained (some of the new types will take sun)
Best Cultivars: It's hard to say; almost all are good
How to Start: Take cuttings in fall and overwinter or start seeds in early spring
When to Transplant: After frost
Use: Beds, planters, pots

Here are the some of the finest of all bedding plants for the Southern flower garden. The plants are beautiful, and the flowers are beautiful. What else could you want? They have no particular insect or disease problems. You can buy a few plants and take cuttings to get many more. All in all, it is one plant you really should grow!

The *I. Wallerana*, which is the most common Impatiens grown, normally takes some shade, especially against the hot afternoon sun, but the hybrids of *I. lineari-folia* from New Guinea do best in full sun. They are also interesting with their variegated foliage and more erect habit of growth.

One of my most exciting overseas adventures was a trip to the highlands of Papua, New Guinea. Near Wabaq I saw my first native New Guinea Impatiens growing beside the road. Here were the parents of these fabulous plants which have become such an integral part of my garden. The only problem which I have found with these marvelous plants is that I do not seem to be able to root them as easily as our common garden Impatiens.

If you do not grow Impatiens in well-drained soil, root rot will gradually cause them to die away. Work the soil with plenty of ground bark or peat moss. If you use the latter, add some limestone because they do best in a moderate pH soil.

If the leaves look droopy in the late afternoon, don't automatically start watering. The soil may already be too wet. Dig into the soil among the plants to see if it is really too dry. If it is, water; if not, let the soil dry and the roots start growing again. Overwatering kills more Impatiens than underwatering.

Three or four weeks ahead of the first expected frost, make a number of cuttings for overwintering. They will root quickly and should be potted in at least a six-inch pot. Grow in good light in the winter where it is warm. Force new growth in the spring with a good fertilizing and make a bunch of cuttings to root for planting in the garden after frost.

LANTANA
Lantana Camara

Class: HHP used as an annual
Height Range: 1 to 3 feet
Colors: Red and yellow, rose and yellow, lilac and cream
Exposure: Full sun
Best Cultivars: Most frequently they come in only mixed colors
How to Start: Inside ahead of spring
When to Transplant: After the ground warms
Use: Tall bedding or background plant

Lantana is an old favorite in the South. The leaves are waxy like an evergreen shrub and the flowers cover the plant until frost. In mild winters a heavy mulch may protect the roots enough for the plant to come back but most often they reseed to produce new plants each year.

Lantana must have full sun and well drained soil. They will not flourish in tight sticky soil.

MARIGOLDS
Tagetes sp. and hybrids

Class: TA
Height Range: Low to tall
Colors: Yellow, orange, mahogany
Exposure: Sun
Best Cultivars: Many, depending on your needs
How to Start: Start seed inside
When to Transplant: After frost
Use: Beds, borders, edging, pot plants, and planters

The Marigolds are most satisfactory and easy to grow. There are now so many sizes, shapes, and color blends that the choice is strictly up to the individual. There are tall ones, short ones, large flowering, and small flowering types. You pay your money and take your choice. Since I find that the seed racks in nurseries and garden supply outlets seldom have the ones I want, I usually get mine from a good catalogue house.

Lantana

Large flowering marigold

Petite dwarf marigold

Large yellow marigolds with medium height

Nicotiana

Orange marigolds with large flowers and medium height

The biggest flowering types are not always the best for the garden. Don't overlook varieties like 'Lemondrop,' with its small yellow flowers in great masses on compact ten-inch plants. They are great for borders.

MONEY PLANT
Lunaria annua

Class: HB
Height Range: 24 to 30 inches
Colors: White, lilac, and purple
Exposure: Full sun
Best Cultivars: *Lunaria annua* 'Alba'
　　　　　　　　Lunaria annua
　　　　　　　　Lunaria annua 'Munstead Purple'
How to Start: To blossom in one year, start in the late summer or early fall in seed trays or pots and set out before cold weather.
When to Transplant: Before cold weather in the fall or in the spring
Use: Background plant and for cutting and drying the unique seed pods which look like a silver coin

The Money Plant has long been planted for the unusual seed pods which, when dried, may be prepared and preserved as a most interesting dried "flower." The center layer of the seed pod is silver in color, and when the outer layers are removed, it resembles a coin.

Money Plant is a true hardy biennial but is most often used in the South as an annual by planting in the fall and thus obtaining flowers the following summer followed by the pods in late summer or fall.

Grow in a sunny spot where the soil is rich and well drained.

NICOTIANA or FLOWERING TOBACCO
Nicotiana alata

Class: TA
Height Range: 12 to 36 inches
Colors: White, red, and purple
Exposure: Full sun to part shade
Best Cultivars: 'Affinis' for taller plants and with most fragrance
　　　　　　　　'Domino' hybrids for dwarf, colorful but less fragrant plants
How to Start: Indoors in seed trays. Do not cover seeds deeply.
When to Transplant: After danger of frost
Use: Tall background or as bedding plants

The white 'Affinis' Flowering Tobacco will give a tuberose fragrance to the garden as well as a sturdy, attractive background plant. It combines well with tall yellow Marigolds, tall purple Heliotrope, pink Hollyhocks and other heavy-blooming, tall-growing plants.

The lower-growing and colored cultivars are perhaps more floriferous, but they do not have the fragrance of the old white 'Affinis.'

Grow in well-prepared and well-drained soil.

PANSY
Viola X Wittrockiana

Class: P, treated as an annual
Height Range: Low
Colors: Blue, yellow, rose, white, red
Exposure: Sun to part shade
Best Cultivars: 'Roggli,' 'Steele's Jumbo,' 'Majestic Giants'
How to Start: Start seed in late August or as soon as it cools a bit. Transplant into small pots and grow in a lightly-shaded spot until time to set in the garden.
When to Transplant: Mid-fall, when the transplants are tough
Use: Beds, planters, pots, and tubs

Pansies are cool-weather plants, ideal for our climate as a late fall, winter, and early spring-flowering plant. As soon as it gets hot, they begin to look awful and should be pulled out of the bed. This is good because it is time to plant summer annuals then anyway.

The great thing is that they will flower all winter, being hardy enough to take all but those cold abominations like in 1983 and 1984–1985. Whenever the weather warms up a bit, here come the Pansies with those cheerful faces telling you that winter isn't all bad here in the South.

Plant them in good soil and fertilize sparingly after the weather cools. In the spring, the leaves may be a bit yellow and another fertilizing with a 6-12-12 or 5-10-15 formula will green them up and give another burst of bloom.

All of us tend to want the biggest of everything and seem to choose the huge-flowered types. Don't succumb to that temptation. Large flowers have a tendency to flop and the bright faces don't look so good. The 'Roggli Swiss Giants' are quite large enough for an excellent show, and the faces are always open and beaming. The colors are excellent, and they also have a blotch, which seems to be bred out of some of the new ones. Who wants a Pansy without a face?

PETUNIA
Petunia X hybrida

Class: TA
Height Range: Low to medium
Colors: Wide range
Exposure: Sun
Best Cultivars: Many
How to Start: Start seed inside
When to Transplant: After frost
Use: Beds and borders

Pansies

Yellow and blue pansies

Yellow pansies

Red hybrid petunias

Large flowering hybrid petunias

Yellow petunias

Commercial breeders have ruined Petunias with all the hybridizing, at least as far as the South is concerned. What used to be a tough, easy-to-grow plant is now a softie, susceptible to almost everything that comes along. This is another case, like roses, where the breeders ignore the South. Maybe since so many from the rest of the country are moving down with us, the breeders will start paying more attention to what we need.

The picture books and catalogues show wonderful flowers on beautiful compact plants. Take a look at these varieties in August here in the South. They are stringy and yellow, have little bloom, and many have died from wilt. In most cases, a Petunia bed in August in the South is nothing to behold.

I know people who do grow good Petunias but they really work at it. Frankly, I quit messing with them a long time ago and am waiting until the South's buying power draws the attention of those who are developing new Petunias. Then perhaps they will breed some with the toughness we need.

Until they do, don't say I didn't warn you!

CALIFORNIA POPPY
Eschscholzia californica

Class: HA
Height Range: Low to medium
Colors: Yellow, orange, red
Exposure: Sun
Best Cultivars: 'Aurantiaca'
How to Start: Start seed inside or seed directly in beds
When to Transplant: After hard freezes
Use: Early spring bedding plant

The California Poppy is one of our best early-flowering annuals. It doesn't like heat so should be started early and enjoyed in the cool months.

SHIRLEY POPPY
Papaver Rhoeas

Class: HA
Height Range: 24 to 30 inches
Colors: White, red, and salmon
Exposure: Full sun
Best Cultivars: 'Sweet Briar,' double pink
How to Start: Start in trays in the late summer and set in the garden before cold or seed directly into well prepared beds at the same time. May also be started inside in the winter.
When to Transplant: In the fall before frost or in the spring after heavy freezes
Use: Tall bedding plant or for cut flowers

I have grown Shirley Poppies for many years along with 'Silver Puff' Hollyhocks and Heliotrope. They are a little tricky to transplant so it is best to sow directly in well prepared garden soil.

Double-flowering Portulaca

Sweet Briar double Shirley poppy

America Salvia planted for hummingbirds

Bonfire Salvia, medium height

Purple Salvia

St. John's Fire Salvia

Perennial Salvia, Salvia farinacea

Bright Eye Periwinkle

White Periwinkle

Rocket hybrid Snapdragons

Shirley Poppies are cool weather plants and should be planted to flower as early in the spring as possible. Their spring and early summer flowers are spectacular but when it gets hot they become pretty ratty and I remove them from the garden.

PORTULACA or MOSS ROSE
Portulaca grandiflora

Class: TA
Height Range: Low
Colors: White, red, pink, orange
Exposure: Sun
Best Cultivars: Doubles
How to Start: Start seed inside or seed directly in late spring when the ground warms
When to Transplant: When the air is warm
Use: Beds

Portulaca will grow in sorry soil and full, hot sun. It is a plant for us to know about because we all have places like that. It is unusual because its foliage is like a succulent and the flowers are set in great profusion over the interesting plant.

Since it likes hot weather, plant it after the nights warm up.

SALVIA or SCARLET SAGE
Salvia splendens

Class: P, treated as a tender annual
Height Range: Low to tall
Colors: Red, flame, white, purple
Exposure: Sun
Best Cultivars: Many good ones which are usually chosen for the height desired, since they all bloom profusely
How to Start: Start seed inside
When to Transplant: After danger of frost
Use: Beds, occasionally as borders, or even as edging

Everybody needs Salvia if only to attract hummingbirds. But it has many other excellent attributes. The plants grow fast, start blooming early, continue to bloom until frost, and have few if any problems, except that bad drainage ruins them.

I always grow a block of Salvia in my garden, for the bright flowers really make it a wonderful place to be. I like to plant the old 'Bonfire' cultivar for height in the back, then 'St. John's Fire' in front of that, and one of the real dwarfs in front of that. We really have the hummingbirds everyday.

Salvia has few needs other than good drainage and moderately rich soil. If you keep it fertilized and the old seed heads popped off, yours will bloom until long after the Hummingbirds have left for the far South.

Salvia farinacea is a perennial form of Salvia which is widely used both as an annual and perennial here in the South. The flowers are not as spectacular as *Salvia splendens* but are quite showy and make a beautiful backdrop for Dwarf Marigolds, Vinca, and other bright colored low-growing plants. The gray-green foliage is clean and attractive.

Salvia farinacea does best in bright sunny locations but will take some high shade.

SNAPDRAGON
Antirrhinum majus

Class: P, usually treated as an annual
Height Range: Low to tall
Colors: White, red, pink, yellow, bronze
Exposure: Sun
Best Cultivars: 'Rocket'
How to Start: Start seed inside in January to have plants to set as soon as it stops freezing
When to Transplant: After hard freezes
Use: Beds

Snapdragons are great! These wonderful plants can be grown successfully in the South if you use a heat-resistant type like the 'Rocket' hybrids and you start early. The best bloom is always in the early spring.

I start snaps early, get them in the garden as soon as the hardest freezes have passed, and let them bloom until they get sparse and somewhat ratty-looking. Then I cut them back and let them rest awhile, and they will start a new burst of growth in the late summer and produce excellent fall blooms. Give them some 5-10-15 when you see a burst of growth and they will blossom better in the fall.

STOCK
Matthiola incana

Class: HA, HHA, HB
Height Range: 12 inches to 30 inches
Colors: Red, pink, lavender, white
Exposure: Sun
Best Cultivars: Trysomic types (more doubled)
How to Start: Inside in seed flats and transplant
When to Transplant: After hard freezes
Use: Early beds

Stocks have much appeal in the early Southern garden for many types bloom quickly and continue flowering until the hot days of May and June. Their double flowers give some of the best color possible for the spring garden. The newer trysomic Stock types are stronger and more double than the older types. For us, they are all used as annuals despite some types being listed as biennials.

Grow Stock in rich, well drained soil and in full sun. Since their growing time occurs in the rainy season, drainage is most important. Many gardeners raise (crown) their beds to give more drainage to this type of plant.

Even those types listed as half-hardy (HHA) are best started in January inside, potted into three- or four-inch pots or cell packs and grown until they are strong enough to set outside when the weather moderates.

SWEET PEA
Lathyrus odoratus

Class: HA
Height Range: Climbing type, 10 feet; bush type, 24 inches
Colors: White, blue, lavender, orange, scarlet, pink
Exposure: Sun
Best Cultivars: 'Knee-Hi'
How to Start: From seed in bed
When to Transplant: Winter
Use: Early beds

I miss the wonderful Sweet Peas that people in the South once had. The new types are much easier since they don't require a place to climb or a Sweet Pea fence to cling to, and we should grow them more.

The new bush types are wonderful and will stand on their own in the garden. They will blossom very early and will be gone by the time the heat really sets in.

Start during a mild spell in January or February, planting in a deep, 8- to 10-inch trench into the bottom of which you have placed a layer of cattle manure. Cover the seed only two or three inches. As the young seedlings grow, fill in the trench. This makes them stocky and tough. Side-dress with a 6-12-12 or 5-10-15 after the trench is filled.

SWEET WILLIAM
Dianthus barbatus

Class: HB
Height Range: Most from 12 to 18 inches
Colors: Reds, whites, pinks, and bicolors
Exposure: Full sun
Best Cultivars: 'Indian Carpet'
　　　　　　　　Common double mixed
How to Start: In seed trays in the fall
When to Transplant: Transplant to the garden before hard freezes occur
Use: Bedding

The Sweet William is an old Southern favorite for late spring and early summer flowers. It seldom lasts into the hottest part of the summer, so it should be looked on as an annual and removed when it becomes unsightly.

VINCA, PERIWINKLE or JEWEL PLANT
Catharanthus roseus

Class: TA
Height Range: Low to medium
Colors: White, white with red eye, rose, pink, salmon
Exposure: Sun to light shade
Best Cultivars: 'Bright Eyes,' 'Polka Dot'
How to Start: Start seed inside
When to Transplant: After frost and when weather warms
Use: Bedding

This is an ideal Southern summer flowering plant. It has rich, glossy green foliage, masses of flowers, and few problems. It grows and grows, blooms and blooms, and always has a cool green appearance under its blanket of flowers. You will have flowers galore from late spring until frost in the fall.

ZINNIA
Zinnia elegans

Class: TA
Height Range: Low to tall
Colors: White (kind of dirty looking), chartreuse, yellow, gold, purple, pink, red, and orange
Exposure: Sun
Best Cultivars: Many; choose for height and flower size
How to Start: Start inside or direct seed
When to Transplant: After ground is warm
Use: Bedding, borders, and planters

Many gardeners would just as soon abandon their plantings as to miss having some Zinnias. They do well in our heat but must be watched for mildew. Plant as the air gets warm and keep fertilized for continued growth and bloom.

There are so many Zinnias from which to choose that my best advice is to read the descriptions and find the ones which fit into your planting scheme.

Cactus flowered Zinnia

Red Zinnia

GROWING BIENNIALS IN THE SOUTH

I do not treat biennials as truly separate from annuals, for in the South they may be grown from seed to bloom in one full year by planting them at the proper time. Hardy biennials are the ones to choose. It is difficult to get good blossoms from tender biennials. It is really possible only when you have a greenhouse or hot bed.

The trick to the growing of biennials in one year is to fool them into thinking it is two years, or more appropriately, two seasons. Do this by starting hardy biennial seed in late summer and early fall in seed trays or seed beds. When they are tough enough to handle, pot them individually in a 3- or 4-inch pot. Grow them for four to six weeks or until they are strong and stocky. Now you may plant them in the right garden location where they will overwinter and begin heavy growth again in the spring.

An alternative method which usually works satisfactorily is to start the seed in January in a greenhouse or hot bed. Transplant them into 3- or 4-inch pots when they are tough enough to handle. As soon as the danger of heavy freezes is past, plant these potted biennials in your garden spot.

Both of these methods will produce plants which will blossom during the spring and summer of the current year.

The first method suggested is best for the spring and early summer biennials; the alternative method is satisfactory for summer and fall biennials.

The first method produces the best overall results for all blooming seasons, however. The only problem would be in cases of very cold winters when even our normally hardy biennials might be damaged. A good mulch over the dormant roots, after the tops have died down, will take them through the worst of Southern winters.

Some biennials like Foxglove and Money Plant will reseed themselves, and the colony will act as if it were perennial. These colonies should be worked sparingly and lightly when the seedlings can be easily seen. Reseeding biennials should always be planted in the best garden soil so that you do not need to work the soil each year.

CHOOSING BIENNIALS TO GROW

Some biennials were described along with annuals. I suggest you check the descriptions of annuals for the details. I have found the biennial Hollyhock, Foxglove, and Lunaria to be particularly easy to keep as colonies here in the South.

Hollyhocks

GROWING HARDY PERENNIALS IN THE SOUTH

How wonderful the idea sounds! Beautiful flowering plants coming forth each year to give the garden the beauty and liveliness we all want, without the bother of digging the bed and planting new plants each year! Perennial flowers have a great appeal to most gardeners. For many perennials, the "press report" is accurate. They can be planted, maintained, and kept for years with little bother. Others, however, may be as much trouble as annuals and biennials are.

PERENNIAL GROWING REQUIREMENTS

Perennials fall into three groups with different site and soil preparation requirements.

Group 1—Trouble-Free Perennials

The first group includes the tough, trouble-free plants which are almost indestructible and will survive the most unpleasant conditions.

Plant these perennials in the exposure mentioned with their descriptions. The soil range is so broad that you do not need to worry unless really tight, sticky situations need correction. Break up the soil with a spade or tiller. Add humus if the soil is heavy clay, and perlite if the drainage is not good. Use a 5-10-15 or a 6-12-12 fertilizer when planting.

Group 2—Easy-To-Grow Perennials

This group includes plants that take no more or less care than the annuals and biennials described previously. These perennials take a wide range of soils, and the spot should be chosen mainly for their exposure requirements. The soil should be better than for Group 1, and drainage should be good. Prepare the beds the same as you would for annuals.

Group 3—Other Perennials For The South

The third group includes specialty perennials which should be grown with the full knowledge that their needs are explicit and must be met for decent results.

Hosta grows well in shade

Place these perennials in the right exposure and prepare the soil especially well. Drainage, fertility of the soil, and the pH should be correct for them to survive and perform well.

Prepare the beds as for annuals, but be sure that the drainage is good. Add more perlite and crown the bed. Have pH tests made on the soil and add limestone to raise the pH if a more neutral or alkaline soil is needed.

This group of perennials thrives on humus. Dehydrated cattle or sheep manure, peat moss, and ground bark are excellent ingredients.

Many of the perennials in this group need cooler conditions than the South normally has. Planting in morning sun rather than afternoon sun will help them survive.

PLANTING HARDY PERENNIALS

All the perennials to be considered make clumps and are grown either from seeds or from divisions of the clumps.

Growing Perennials From Seed

The seed of hardy perennials may be planted twice a year, in the early fall outside in seed beds or trays, or in the winter in seed trays in greenhouses, cold frames or seed trays in a bright, sunny window inside.

Fall is the best time to plant seed, for the seedlings will develop rapidly after potting and may soon be planted into the well-prepared garden spot. After the tops have been killed by frost or freezes, mulch the bed for winter protection. In the spring, when the weather begins to moderate, peek under the mulch to see if your young plants are sprouting. If they are, remove the mulch from over the plants, work the bed lightly around the growing plants, and fertilize with a 5-10-15 or 6-12-12 formula.

Growing Perennials From Divisions

After the clumps mature, the plants may become crowded and their performance diminishes. You should divide the clumps and reset the new plants. This is usually done every three to five years, though some plants, like Hosta and Liriope (also Ophiopogon), will grow for many, many years without the need for dividing.

Dig the clumps with a spade or spading fork and separate the sprouts from the clump by pulling or cutting apart. Try to separate into divisions of at least three good shoots, except in the case of Chrysanthemums, where a single healthy shoot is all that is necessary.

At the time of dividing, rework the bed after you have removed all the plants. If only a few clumps in a bed are being divided, work the area from which the clumps are removed with a spading fork or spade. Add humus, lime if needed, and dehydrated cow manure to enrich the soil. Add perlite if the soil has become tight and sticky.

The time of the year for dividing perennials will vary, depending on the type. I prefer doing this in the fall whenever possible, because then

A. Perennials should be divided when clumps are crowded and flowers become smaller.

B. Dig the clump and wash the soil off the roots. Identify the divisions by the old stalks or possibly some new shoots.

C. Cut the divisions apart so that there is a healthy shoot or shoots with each group of roots. Replant carefully.

the new divisions will have the winter and early spring to develop strong new roots. Chrysanthemums, however, may still be blooming very late in the fall, and in that case, it is better to divide in the spring.

Do spring dividing as early as possible but after the danger of hard freezing is past and before the sprouts become too large.

The best way to obtain these plants is to purchase plant divisions from a plant outlet or through a catalogue. This is less expensive than waiting for plants growing in a container, and in my opinion, it is better because you can plant earlier with better results in plant performance and bloom.

Divisions can usually be found in plant outlets in the late fall (late October and November) and in the early spring (late February, March, and April). Catalogue purchase and shipments are from fall through spring.

Potted or container-grown perennials are usually found after the weather warms and the plants are actively growing. Handle them carefully and grow them with great care. Pay particular attention to watering, because the heavy growth will require ample moisture. The first year's performance of potted, growing perennials is dependent on how well the bed is prepared and how well you provide moisture during the dry periods of May. Follow these tips on planting divisions.

- Prepare the soil well.
- Add manure, fertilizer, and lime, if needed.
- Plant with the crown right at the level of the bed. Do not bury the shoots.
- Mulch around the plants to conserve moisture.

ALL ABOUT PERENNIALS FOR THE SOUTH

Group 1: Trouble-Free Perennials

We have already talked about several of these plants in other sections. Liriope, for instance, is an easy-to-grow perennial which lasts for years. It is a herbaceous perennial. Daylilies are another almost carefree perennial. The following list contains some plants which we seldom think of in the same context with the plants of an English perennial garden, but perennials they are, just the same.

AJUGA
Ajuga reptans

This widely-used ground cover grows in shady areas and even fairly moist soil. It creeps along the ground by means of runners. The blossom is generally a spike of blue flowers in the spring, though there are pink and white cultivars. Some cultivars also have foliage which is quite bronze, and some have variegated green and white leaves.

Ajuga is started from divisions, but most often is found in nurseries as small potted plants or clumps in larger containers.

DAYLILY
Hemerocallis sp.

Daylilies are especially good perennials for the South. They are extremely tough and tenacious, and a well-established clump will last for years and years. Grow most cultivars in full sun to light shade, though some are advertised as taking more shade. Grow them in shade with caution because heavy shading eliminates heavy blooming.

Daylilies will grow in good or bad soil, needing little care. Of course a well-tilled and prepared bed will always result in the best plants and flowers.

Hyperion, the Lemon Lily, is perhaps the best one of all. Its peak of bloom is in mid-summer, with clusters of large, bright yellow flowers. The flowers may also be cut and used in arrangements. The best method is to cut the stalks with buds which are just beginning to open. They will open into glorious flowers in your arrangement.

Daylilies are particularly effective on banks where it is impossible to grow grass. Prepare the soil well; set divisions on staggered two-foot centers; apply a mulch between the plants to prevent washing, and keep them growing heavily with a 5-10-15 fertilizer. Soon the bank will be filled with strong, healthy, blooming-size plants which will continue to hold the soil and cover your problem bank. To me it certainly beats junipers!

Hemerocallis are started from divisions found in nurseries during the dormant season or container-grown clumps found throughout the year.

Ajuga

Ferns are beautiful in shady areas

Hosta in flower

Variegated Hosta

Shady flower bed with Hosta

❦ FERNS
Many different genera and species

No discussion of plants for the garden should omit Ferns. Strictly speaking, these plants are in a different taxonomic area from the flowering, seed-producing herbaceous perennials which are our focus at the present. However, these plants are extremely important and many act as perennials by being killed to the ground each winter and regrowing healthy, vigorous fronds the next growing season.

Use ferns in poorly drained, deeply shaded spots where few other plants will grow. Good soil preparation, high humus content, a moderately low pH, and ample moisture will give ferns what they need to grow well.

There are any number of native Southern ferns which may be grown in the garden. Catalogues list hardy ferns such as the 'Toothed Wood Fern,' the 'Sword Fern,' and 'Christmas Fern,' which are worthy additions to the shaded garden.

The Climbing Fern, **Lygodium,** is one mentioned with the Vines which is particularly attractive. It will take a moderate amount of sun and should be considered as an interesting and unusual addition to your plantings.

❦ HOSTA or PLANTAIN LILY
Hosta sp.

The Hosta is a magnificent group of herbaceous perennials which grow in varying degrees of light, from moderate to heavy shade. These plants are grown primarily for their foliage. There are species and cultivars with varying foliage shapes, from a large rounded leaf to almost a strap leaf. Some are green- and white-leaved, others rich green, and a few have a blue-green cast.

Hostas grow in a wide range of soils, but prefer moderate drainage. Tight, sticky soil will reduce the growth rate and the beauty of the clump even though the plant may survive such conditions.

Many of the Hostas will form seeds freely, and a good method of increasing your plantings is to leave a few seed stalks on the plant after the flowers have finished blooming. Harvest the drying pods when they crack open and remove the seeds. Store them in a loosely-capped container or "baggie" in a cool place. Plant them in seed trays in January, potting the seedlings in three or four pots as soon as they are tough enough to handle. Keep them growing well in a bright spot inside or in cold frames or a greenhouse until after the danger of frost, when you can set them in their garden spot.

The variegated Hostas, however, do not seed freely, and some seem never to seed at all. I have clumps of Hosta which are almost twenty years old and are still the most beautiful, cool-looking plants you can imagine, growing in an area where I have never succeeded with anything else except Ferns.

The common way to start Hostas is from divisions which may be found in nurseries from late October until spring, or from potted or container-grown clumps which are found during the growing season.

❧ LIRIOPE AND OPHIOPOGON
Liriope Muscari and *L. spicata, Ophiopogon japonicus*

These two perennial grass-like plants are propagated by divisions or may be found in heavily-growing clumps in containers at most nurseries.

❧ PACHYSANDRA
Pachysandra terminalis

Pachysandra is propagated by divisions found in nurseries during the winter or growing in containers in the spring and early summer.

❧ THRIFT or MOSS PINK
Phlox subulata

Thrift is so common in much of the South that it seems almost native. It is widely grown on dry banks and other areas where little else is happy. It thrives and spreads over almost impossible areas, giving a matted appearance when it has covered well.

Thrift is so common that it is belittled, especially when the hot pink or lavender cultivars are grown. Yet, here is a plant that will survive where others fail, and there are much-improved cultivars which range from a pure white to a true blue with fair reds and pinks in between.

Plant Thrift in the early spring after the ground is not prone to freezing. Fertilize after blossoming so that it will spread rapidly over the area. In the mid-summer, after its burst of growth has finished, Thrift may become a bit ratty. Don't mess with it or you may cause die-out. It's merely resting.

Group 2: Easy-To-Grow Perennials

These perennials grow with little more care than our common annuals. Actually, we should consider them in the same breath because there is little point in segregating these fine plants merely because their botany is different.

I know many excellent gardeners who use these intermingled with annuals, either working the soil around them or lifting the clumps in the late winter, working the entire bed in preparation for annuals, and resetting the clumps as if they were new annual plants.

❧ BASKET OF GOLD ALYSSUM
Aurinia saxatilis (Alyssum saxatile)

The Basket of Gold Alyssum produces heavy, foot-high growth on which a mass of yellow flowers form in the spring. Give it plenty of sun and good drainage.

BELAMCANDA or BLACKBERRY LILY
Belamcanda chinensis

Belamcanda is not frequently used in the Southern garden. This is a pity, for it is quite attractive and very easy to grow. Some authors list it with the Iris because it is easily confused with bearded Iris when it is not in bloom. Belamcanda, however, does not make the heavy rhizome which is the case with the bearded Iris.

Belamcandas are easily propagated from seeds which are set profusely and are somewhat attractive if left on the plant. Seeds may be taken anytime after they turn black and may be planted immediately after drying. I start them in seed trays and overwinter the small plants in a freeze-free place where they can get plenty of light. Then I set them in the garden the following spring.

These unusual plants grow well in full sun and well drained, rich garden soil. They should be set out in the early spring and may blossom the first year from seed. As the clump becomes larger, the blossoms are more profuse and very showy.

Belamcanda has many variations in flower color which also makes a planting attractive.

CANDYTUFT
Iberis sempervirens

The perennial Candytuft is an excellent border, bedding, or rock garden plant for sunny to lightly-shaded areas. It has a mass of white blossoms in the spring which literally cover the plant. After it blossoms, shear off the drying seed pods and fertilize to get good new growth. For the least disruption of bloom, divide immediately after blossoming has finished.

GARDEN CHRYSANTHEMUM (MUM)
Chrysanthemum X

The garden mum is ideally suited to the South if you choose the hardy cultivars. Most of these are the cushion types which grow from twelve to thirty inches tall and are covered with masses of flowers of many colors depending on the cultivar. There are bright yellow, gold, maroon red, bronze, lavender pink, and white cultivars which do well for us, blooming profusely in the fall until heavy freezes occur.

The tall "football" and "spider" mums are best left to Chrysanthemum specialists because they need staking, correct pinching, and extra good culture to perform well.

It is best to start Chrysanthemums from divisions. Lift the clump in the spring after you see a number of small shoots appearing. When these shoots are three to four inches tall, carefully remove each shoot with a number of roots and

Thrift

Perennial garden Pinks

Bushy, well-grown Chrysanthemums

Chrysanthemum that has been pinched

Large flowered perennial Hibiscus grown from seed

Iberis, perennial Candytuft

Purple Coneflower

reset them in well-prepared soil. In some years when the weather is moderate after the first hard freeze, these shoots may also appear, and it is a good time to divide.

In the spring, nurseries will have small rooted plants for sale. This is the least expensive way to start a Chrysanthemum planting when you have no clumps to divide. Nowadays nurseries offer large potted mums in the fall. Though this is expensive, it is a good way to have instant color with very little effort. If grown well, these heavy plants will produce many shoots the following spring from which you can get large numbers of plants.

GROWING CHRYSANTHEMUMS

Chrysanthemums need some attention during their growth period. They need good garden soil, plenty of drainage, and lots of sun. Fertilize with a 5-10-15 or 6-12-12 formula.

When the young shoot reaches six inches, remove the tip (this is called pinching"). This slows the shoot growth upward, starts branching, and keeps the plant from becoming leggy. As each branch reaches four to six inches, pinch it just as you did the main shoot. Continue to pinch until early July, when the plant will be well-branched, stocky, and ready to start setting buds. Pinching too late may reduce the number of flower buds for fall.

CHRYSANTHEMUM PROBLEMS

Most garden mum problems are related to growth, though aphids, spider mites, and leafhoppers may sometimes cause problems that you should control as soon as you discover them.

Tall, leggy plants with few basal leaves result from crowding and indicate that the clump needs dividing.

❦ DIANTHUS or GARDEN PINKS
Dianthus plumarius

The Garden Pinks are a long-lasting group of Dianthus which form low mounding plants 12 to 15 inches in height. The foliage is gray-green and the flowers are rose-red, pink, and white with a delightful scent. The flowers appear mainly in late spring and early summer. This is a wonderful rock garden plant because it nestles between and over rocks with great ease.

Pinks grow well in full sun to light shade but do best in well-drained soil, perhaps on the dry side.

❦ HIBISCUS or ROSE MALLOW
Hibiscus Moscheutos

The hardy Hibiscus is a wonderful source of spectacular blooms for the summer. Older cultivars are planted from divisions, while newer, fast-developing types may be grown from seed. 'Southern Belle' is a popular cultivar to be started inside from seed and transplanted into the garden as the ground warms. It will blossom freely from early summer until fall and has large eight- to ten-inch blossoms in colors ranging from red to pink to white. The plants of 'Southern Belle' grow to three feet and spread to about the same.

These Hibiscus are subject to attacks from a green worm which devastates the foliage. Spray or dust with bacillus thurengiensis (Dipel or Thuricide), which is a safe and effective control.

PURPLE CONEFLOWER
Echinacea purpurea

The Purple Coneflowers are easy-to-grow sunny-spot plants which will last for years if kept clean of mildew. They do best in rich, well-drained soil with good air movement. They will easily attain a height of three or four feet and bloom through the middle and late summer months.

There are cultivars that vary from the common purple with a black eye and include white and pink forms.

BLACK-EYED SUSAN
Rudbeckia sp.

This large group of plants is ideal as Southern perennials. In fact, some of the Rudbeckias can be seen naturalized through much of the South. They are easy to grow in any well-drained soil and will tolerate some light shade.

My personal preferences are the Gloriosa Daisies which have large golden yellow flowers. There are both single and double forms, though I find the singles more pleasing and more daisy-like.

SHASTA DAISY
Chrysanthemum X Superbum

The Shasta Daisy has long been a favorite of Southerners. It is easy to grow and will quickly expand from an individual transplanted seedling or division into a massive clump full of flowers during the mid-summer.

There are a number of cultivars with a range in height from about eighteen to forty-eight inches. There are also semi-double and double cultivars in addition to the more common single form. But the Shasta is, after all, a daisy, and so to me the large single white flower with the prominent yellow center is the best to grow. In this favorite group are many cultivars with height and size variations, which gives you a wide range from which to choose. 'Angel Wings,' one cultivar of note, forms a beautiful clump with a plant height of about thirty inches.

Group 3: Other Perennials for the South

The perennials described in detail above are the ones most commonly grown in the Southern garden. The list now broadens tremendously into the types which are grown widely through much of the country. This group includes such favorites as Aster, Astilbe, Bleeding Heart, Delphinium, Dicentra, Columbine, Lavender, Monarda, Rosemary, Perennial Salvia, Stokesia, and many you will find listed in catalogues specializing in these plants. Their omission from the above lists may disappoint many who have had success with them, and in no way indicates that they should be avoided.

If you are a newcomer to perennial-growing, start with those which I have described in Groups 1 and 2. As you accumulate successes, then charge forth into new worlds of the harder-to-grow types. Being successful with seldom-grown plants adds tremendous interest and sets your garden apart from the run-of-the-mill. It is at this point that gardening becomes most meaningful.

These less widely-used perennials can be grown if you have an understanding of their special needs and of the extra attention they must have. The perennial societies in many Southern cities are excellent sources of information for you. Botanical gardens often have perennial areas, which can provide inspiration for the viewer.

There are other good possibilities for you to try as you expand your perennial plantings. I list a few here for you to consider.

Large-flowering, tall-growing Phlox

Delphinium   Columbine

GROUP 3: OTHER PERENNIALS FOR THE SOUTH

COMMON NAME AND BOTANICAL NAME	HEIGHT	EXPOSURE	COLOR	CLASS	NOTES
ASTILBE Astilbe sp.	15 in.	Sun	Red, pink, white	2	Bright feather flowers
BALLOON FLOWER Platycodon grandiflorus	18 to 36 in.	Sun/Part shade	White, pink, blue	3	Unusual flowers
BEE BALM Monarda didyma	24 to 30 in.	Sun/Part shade	Red, pink, white	2	Needs moisture to bloom well
BLEEDING HEART Dicentra sp.	12 to 24 in.	Sun or shade	White, red, pink	3	Grow with care
COLUMBINE Aquilegia sp.	18 to 36 in.	Part shade	Mixed	3	Beware of leaf miners
DELPHINIUM Delphinium sp.	Various	Morning sun	White, blue, purple, pink	3	Grow with care
GERBERA DAISY Gerbera Jamesonii	18 in.	Sun to light shade	Pastels	2	Somewhat tender
PAINTED DAISY Pyrethrum sp. and Chrysanthemum sp.	24 to 36 in.	Sun	Red, pink, white	3	Needs moisture
SEDUM Sedum spectabile	15 to 18 in.	Full sun	Various reds	2	Grow in well-drained dry soil

CHAPTER 2

BULBS FOR THE SOUTH

The perennials we have looked at so far are those grown from seed or divisions of clumps. Though these are the ones we commonly refer to as perennials for the garden, there is a whole group of perennials which we use very effectively and commonly call bulbous plants.

These herbaceous perennials are some of our most interesting plants. Instead of dying to the ground each winter and returning from a crown and roots, they go through their cycle and lie dormant as an underground storage organ until a growth bud resprouts during the next growing cycle. Some, like Tulips and Narcissus, do not follow the regular pattern of growing during the growing season and lying dormant when it is freezing and cold; instead, they grow during the colder months, blossom and grow during the spring, and lie dormant in the ground during the summer.

These plants can be classified by the type of underground storage organ they have:

- **True Bulbs**, like Narcissus, Tulips, and Lilies
- **Corms**, like Gladiolus
- **Tubers**, like Caladiums and Elephant Ears
- **Rhizomes**, like Cannas
- **Tuberous roots**, like Dahlias

The garden should contain an assortment of these fabulous plants because they add variations of color, bloom, leaf shape and form, and growth habit which cannot be found elsewhere. Most of the bulbous-type plants

59

Tender Caladium bulbs must be lifted and stored each fall.

are thought of as blossoming plants but this is a mistake; some of the best leaf colors and forms may be found here. Caladiums, with their delightful variegation, and Elephant Ears, with their tropical appearance, will add much to your plantings.

One of the advantages of growing bulbous-type plants is that you may overcome hardiness problems easily by lifting the tender storage organs before frost or freezing temperatures reach them in the ground. Since these organs are designed for dormant storage, they may be overwintered easily in a protected place without the bother of constant watering or other growth problems that afflict tender perennials that are overwintered inside or even in a greenhouse.

Another advantage of growing bulbous plants is that many have their flowering and growth period before the leaves appear on deciduous trees. Therefore their place in the garden may be sunny, whereas later on, when the leaves come out overhead, their place might be too shady.

A tremendous number of these bulbous plants may be used in our gardens. Don't be afraid to try new ones that you hear about. Just be sure that you understand the growth cycle and whether the storage organ is hardy to cold, frosty, or freezing soil.

THE CYCLE OF BULBOUS-TYPE PLANTS

Understanding why bulbous plants are different is important in understanding how they are to be grown and handled. Like all seed-bearing plants, they originally started as seedlings which grew, produced flowers, and started storing food in the underground storage organ. When this cycle of growth finished, the top died to the underground organ, and the plant stayed dormant as a "bulb" until nature triggered the new cycle of growth and bloom. The exact pattern of growth and bloom varies from type to type, some having blossoms before leaves, others blossoming as the leaves appear, and others after the leaves have died down.

It is important to understand these patterns because they determine the manner in which the plant must be grown. Narcissus, for instance, produce flowers as the leaves appear and the leaves continue to grow after the flowers have finished. If the leaves are cut off immediately after flowering, there is no time to produce food to store in the bulb for the next year's bloom and growth. Many gardeners have found, to their dismay, that removing the floppy green leaves of Narcissus too soon after bloom results in few blossoms and weak growth the next year. In this case it is necessary to endure the unsightliness of this foliage until it turns yellow and loses its function. Then the bulb is refilled with food for the new cycle, and the bulb lies dormant until triggered into new growth by nature.

CARING FOR BULBOUS-TYPE PLANTS

Actually, we are looking at a plant group that has a tremendous range of growing needs. There are sunny location types, some for rather deep shade, many that grow well in natural areas, and others that must be pampered like the harder-to-grow perennials. Some, like the Elephant Ears, will even grow in rather wet soil.

The best rule is to grow bulbous-type plants in the same type of soil conditions that I described for other perennials. For most, give them plenty of sun, well-prepared soil that drains well, and ample nutrients to

Red and yellow tulips

grow properly, and keep the insects and diseases under control. Sound familiar? Well, these are the rules I have noted over and over, and they apply here just as they apply to almost all other plants. If you need further information, go back to the general section on Soil Preparation found in Volume I.

HOW TO FERTILIZE BULBOUS-TYPE PLANTS

These plants, like all others we have seen, need the three basic nutrients, nitrogen, phosphorous, and potash, to grow properly. The fact that they spend a great deal of their effort producing the underground storage organ does, however, necessitate changing the ratio of these three somewhat. There are many special bulb fertilizers found in garden shops. They are blended to give a higher ratio of phosphorous and potash to nitrogen than are fertilizers blended for growing plants, like grass, for green leaves.

I like a fertilizer with a 6-12-12 or 5-10-15 formula for growing bulbous-type plants. When planting, use about 2 lbs. per 100 square feet of bed area. After the plantings are established, use about 1 lb. each subsequent year when the foliage is actively growing and storing food in the storage organ.

Most bulbs grow best in a pH range of 6.0 to 6.8. Many soils will need lime to raise the pH to that level. A soil test is an excellent way to determine how much lime is needed.

HOW TO PLANT BULBOUS-TYPE PLANTS

Growing bulbs is like growing all other plants. The general rules for good soil preparation, for the right sun exposure, and for the right fertilizer are very important. In addition, it is important to know the proper planting depth for each type grown. Unfortunately, this varies in different sections of the country. Planting depth in the South may be quite different from planting depth in the North. Beware, and follow Southern rules, not those in books or planting charts written for the country in general. I will give you the correct planting depth in the descriptions of the various types. The general rule of true bulb-planting depth is three times the greatest diameter of the bulb for large bulbs and four times for small bulbs. In the absence of specific information otherwise, use this rule. Corms, tubers, rhizomes, and the others must be planted according to their specific requirements.

Always plant true bulbs and corms with the growth tip upward. Rhizomes, tubers, and tuberous roots should be examined to find the vegetative buds so as to have them pointed upward, even though the structure may be lying on its side.

HOW TO DIG BULBOUS-TYPE PLANTS

Many of these plants will last in the ground for years without needing to be lifted, specifically those that are hardy enough to withstand the cold in the ground during the winter, like Narcissus and Crocus. Others like Dahlias, which are tender, must be dug each fall before cold weather and stored in a protected place while the ground is subject to frost and freezing.

Those left in the ground for several years may become crowded and the clumps so large that separating is necessary to bring them back into

Bulb planters are useful tools.

vigorous growth and bloom. You must do this at the right time in the growth cycle, after the maximum food has been stored in the underground organ.

A few bulbs, like many Tulips, "play out" after a few years in the ground. It is usually not worth trying to dig, separate, and reset them. Rework the bed, discard the small bulbs which you will find underground, and start a new planting with fresh bulbs.

True bulbs and corms are easily separated by gently pulling the smaller bulblets away from the main bulb. Cut tubers and rhizomes into pieces which have at least one "eye" or growth bud on each piece. Tuberous roots, as of Dahlias, may be cut apart but each piece must have a part of the stem or crown left attached to it.

HOW TO STORE BULBOUS-TYPE PLANTS

Each of these bulbous-type plants has its own specific storage requirements. Some, like Tulips and Narcissus, must be stored in a cool, dry location until they are replanted. Too high storage temperature will affect the flower bud inside the bulb and may prevent good flowering.

Store Caladiums and Elephant Ears at rather warm temperatures, between 60 and 65 degrees, since they may rot in a colder storage temperature. Cannas, Dahlias, Peonies, and most true bulbs perform best when they are stored between 40 and 50 degrees.

All these bulbous organs should be cleaned thoroughly after digging. Remove all soil from the organ, even washing if necessary. Those which may be stored air dry should be dried and stored in loose mesh bags or in trays. Those that should be stored extremely dry, like Dahlias, should be packed in dry vermiculite in boxes. Those, like Peonies and Cannas, that need a slight amount of moisture to prevent the buds from drying out should be stored in lightly-dampened peat moss.

ALL ABOUT BULBOUS-TYPE PLANTS
FOR THE SOUTHERN GARDEN

❦ FANCY-LEAVED CALADIUM
Caladium X hortulanum

Tuber-forming Perennial
Showy from spring to fall

The Fancy-Leaved Caladiums provide some of the best color for light to moderate shade. They are excellent in wooded areas, shady beds, and borders. They are easy to grow, requiring only warm ground, plenty of drainage, moderate fertilizing, and supplemental water in extremely dry periods.

Caladiums are native to tropical America and thus do best when the weather is very warm. They will not sprout from the tubers in cold, wet ground, and so it is wise to start them ahead of the season in pots in a warm, sunny place inside.

Caladiums must be dug before cold weather, usually when the first light frost kisses the leaves. Store in a moderately warm, dark place inside where the temperature will not drop below 55 degrees. They store well when packed in dry vermiculite.

Many excellent Caladium cultivars can be found with a range of leaf colors. My favorite is 'Candidum,' the most popular green and white variegated leaf form. The leaves are white with strong green veining. There are also red and greens, and white and reds and many other combinations.

I have seen Caladiums in almost every tropical country where I have been, and in these places I have run across some outstanding cultivars which are not generally seen in Southern garden shops. In the Philippines a friend had a very interesting miniature growing on a shelf outside her house. I asked her where she got it, and she showed me a woodsy spot where she found it growing wild and lifted it for her yard.

❦ CANNA
Canna X generalis

Rhizome-forming Perennial
Summer flowering

Cannas are almost universal in warm countries. I have seen them all over the Mediterranean, east central Africa, the Philippines, Malaysia and even in the highlands of Papua, New Guinea, where there was a beautiful bed in front of the government building. They are widely grown because they are beautiful, tough and virtually pest-free. The Canna is a favorite here in the South because it does well in hot weather and will survive the winter in most areas without lifting and storing. Cannas are also easy to grow!

Cannas do best when planted in full sun and well-prepared soil which has good drainage and is fertilized moderately, especially with manure.

'Candidum,' Fancy Leafed Caladium

Miniature Caladium in the Philippines

Caladiums used as a porch plant

Caladiums are found in many colorful leaf forms.

Caladiums in the garden

Cannas

A bed of cannas

Crocus announce that spring is coming.

Gerrie Hoeck Dahlia

A bed of Dahlias at Floweracres

The many cultivars of Canna include a wide range of height and color. It is wise to choose the cultivar carefully because some, like 'King Humbert,' will grow as tall as six or seven feet, and others, like the 'Pfitzer Dwarfs,' will stay low at about 30 to 48 inches. The color range is red, yellow, orange-scarlet, orange, pink, and creamy white. Most have rich green foliage, though a few have bronze leaves.

Start new plantings in pots inside for early setting or outside about the time you plant sweet potatoes when the ground is warm.

Cannas may become overcrowded after several years in the same spot and should be lifted, separated, and reset. Fall or early spring is a good time for this job. Divide the clumps by cutting the rhizomes apart, being sure that each piece has a vegetative bud from which the new plant can grow. Store fall divisions over the winter in slightly damp peat moss at 45 to 50 degrees and reset the following spring when the ground is warm. Plant Caladiums shallowly with the top of the rhizome barely covered.

 CROCUS
Crocus sp.

Corm-forming Perennial
Spring flowering

The Crocus is one of the first blossoming perennials of the year in the South. The blossoms seem to pop up during each warm spell from January on, giving a hint that we are not eternally damned with cold. They are easy to grow and will last for years in a given spot. I have one small colony which has bloomed triumphantly on a rather sad bank for 20 years.

Plant the corms in the fall in any sunny, well-drained spot where the bright colors will be appreciated. Crocus naturalize easily and the colony will persist despite much abuse.

Crocus are excellent as borders or in front of other flowering plants, especially other spring-flowering bulbs. The most popular is the large Dutch Crocus, *Crocus vernus,* which is one of the spring-flowering types, though you may find other species that will blossom in the late spring or even the fall. The color range of the Dutch Crocus is blue, red, yellow, and white with a few bicolors.

Plant Crocus in the late fall and leave them undisturbed until the colonies are so crowded that the blossoms become sparse. Follow the rule of thumb, and plant at a depth of about three times the greatest diameter of the corm. The planting depth is usually about three inches deep if you have purchased a large, number-one-size corm.

 DAHLIA
Dahlia X

Tuberous-rooted Perennial
Summer flowering

I discussed the small flowering seedling Dahlias with the annuals. They will also make a storage root and may be dug and stored over the winter. I prefer, however, to start them from seed each year since the seedlings are stockier and produce an abundance of bloom.

The large-flowering, tall-growing Dahlias should be started from the tuberous roots. An almost infinite number of these, divided into twelve groups by the American Dahlia Society, include the cactus, peony, formal decorative, ball, pompom, single, and anemone types which are so popular.

The culture of the Dahlia can be very strict, especially when growing for prize-winning flowers. However, the novice may take it easy and grow perfectly beautiful bedding and display flowers with little effort.

Dahlias need a well-prepared bed with plenty of humus and excellent drainage, in addition to abundant sun. Keep them fertilized after they start growing with a low-nitrogen, high-phosphate and potash formula. They do grow tall and should be staked.

Dig the tuberous roots of Dahlias each fall about the time of the first light frost. Cut the stalk off, shake away the excess soil, and dry as a clump. After the Dahlias are thoroughly dry, divide the clump by cutting each tuberous root with a piece of a stem. Store by packing in dry peat moss or vermiculite. The winter storage temperature should be cool, in the 40-degree range.

Plant Dahlia roots on their side, being careful not to injure or break off the piece of the crown from which the new plant will arise. The top of the roots should be about six inches deep.

ELEPHANT EARS
Colocasia esculenta

Tuber-forming Perennial
Showy from late spring until frost

The only Colocasia you will find in the nurseries in this country is the common, large, green-leaved type. This is a great pity, for I have seen many others growing wild in such diverse places as Egypt and the Philippines that are far more attractive than the one we grow. I have also seen pictures of *Colocasia* that were green with white veins. There is a close relative, the *Alocasia,* that I have seen growing wild in the tropics and that has some absolutely beautiful leaf forms. Some *Alocasias,* however, do not make a tuber and thus will probably not be available, at least in the same abundance as the tuber-forming ones and the *Colocasia.*

Until importers of unusual plants get on the ball, we are stuck with the commonly-grown type which isn't bad at all, though it's a bit tiresome. The huge leaves give a tropical effect, and when grown in mass, it will make an excellent background for lower shade-loving flowering plants.

Colocasia will take a great deal of shade though they are quite happy in the full sun. Their main requirement is their need for plenty of moisture. I have seen them being grown with their roots at stream level, yet in the garden they seem to favor rich loose soil with good drainage, provided there is ample moisture. They are heavy feeders and should be fertilized liberally with something like a 10-10-10 fertilizer.

Plant at the same time you plant Caladiums, or when the ground is warm, for Colocasia are of tropical origin and need heat in the soil to sprout and grow well. Plant the tubers two to three inches deep and about two feet apart for best effect. Always dig them in the fall before the ground becomes cold. A touch of frost on the leaves indicates that it is time to dig. Store them dry, in a moderately warm place where the temperature does not go below 50 degrees.

Interestingly enough, these tubers provide food for many people; in the Orient they are prepared as poi. The street vendors sell them in Egypt, where they are also widely eaten as a substitute for potatoes. If you ever have the opportunity of growing some of the other cultivars, you will have something even more worthwhile and interesting.

GLADIOLUS
Gladiolus X

Corm-forming Perennial
Summer flowering

This has never been a favorite garden plant of mine, simply because it is best used as a cut-flower and leaves much to be desired as a bedding or garden flowering plant. This doesn't mean that it should not be planted; rather, watch where you plant them. These are best grown in beds prepared specifically for cut flowers rather than in landscape beds designed for color in the garden.

The Gladiolus plants are stalky and should generally be staked. Plantings must be made in succession in order to have flowers over a long period of time. This is fine if they are grown in an area set aside for this type of plant and not in conjunction with other garden flowers.

Plant Gladiolus as soon as the ground warms and in succession so that you will have an extended blossoming period. Plant the corms at a depth of three to five inches. If strong corms are planted at the deeper figure, they will be stronger and stockier and may even stand without staking. Most cultivars will blossom in about six weeks from the time they sprout. In the South, the corms may overwinter, especially if mulched well, but the best results come from fresh plantings each year made in soil that has been well-prepared and has excellent drainage. Dig at the sign of the first frost, clean the corms thoroughly, and store dry in a cool place.

DUTCH HYACINTH
Hyacinthus orientalis

Bulb-forming Perennial
Spring flowering

The Dutch or Garden Hyacinth is prized for the formal, stiff spring blossoms which come in a number of colors: red, rose-pink, lilac, yellow, and white. They are widely grown as border and bedding plants or may be used in planters or large pots.

Elephant Ears of unusual leaf formation in Cairo, Egypt

Gladiolus

Elephant Ears

Blue Hyacinths

Grape Hyacinths

Louisiana Iris

Golden Lily

'Southern Comfort' Bearded Iris

Dutch Iris

Oriental Iris

Bicolor Bearded Iris

Like most bulbs, they do best in rich, well-drained soil to which has been added a liberal amount of humus and limestone in acid soil. Fertilize with a 6-12-12 or 5-10-15 formula when the flowers begin to fade.

Plant the bulbs in the late fall after the ground is cool. Later planting may result in the flowers appearing on very short stalks. Purchase bulbs as soon as you see them in the garden supply outlets and store them in the bottom of the refrigerator until planting time. If the bulbs lie in a warm store for too long, they may blossom poorly the first year.

I prefer Hyacinths planted in groups of colors or in borders of a single color rather than mixtures, which tend to look snaggle-toothed. The South does not have the luxury of perpetual beds or borders of Hyacinths. Since they usually begin to play out in three or four years, take them up when they grow small and spindly and discard the old bulbs, replanting in the fall with fresh ones.

There are other Hyacinths worth noting. The **Roman Hyacinth**, *Hyacinthus orientalis albulus,* is smaller-growing with looser, less stiff flower spikes. They usually persist in the garden longer than the Dutch Hyacinth.

The **Grape Hyacinth** is not in the same genus but is *Muscari sp.* It does extremely well in the South and will last for many years in the same spot.

All Hyacinth and *Muscari* bulbs should be planted by the rule of thumb, i.e., three times the greatest diameter as the planting depth.

IRIS
Iris sp.

Rhizome- or Bulb-forming Perennials
Spring, summer, and fall flowering, depending on the type

Iris have long been some of the South's favorite and easiest-to-grow perennials. The large rhizomatous **Bearded Iris** have graced Southern gardens for generations with their large "flag" blossoms starting in the late spring and continuing into the summer. The bulb-forming Iris that are most popular are the **Dutch Iris,** *Iris Xiphium,* which are planted in the fall and which blossom after Tulips in the spring.

Other Iris are used, such as the little native *Iris cristata* and the **Japanese Iris,** *Iris Kaempferi* and **Siberian Iris,** *Iris sibirica.* The **Louisiana Iris,** *Iris fulva,* is a favorite for low, wet areas.

By far the most popular type of Iris grown in the South is the **Bearded Iris,** which grows extremely well. This rhizomatous Iris grows best in sun and in well-drained soil which can even be on the poor side.

There are a tremendous number of Bearded Iris cultivars from which to choose. These vary in height and color and thus should be carefully chosen for the effect you wish. They are best used in masses or in groups with other perennials or even annuals. They are long-lasting and will survive in a good spot for years without the need of disturbing except when the clumps become very crowded and the blossom diminishes. Divide at any time except immediately after blossoming or when the ground is subject to freezing. Lift the clumps and carefully cut the rhizomes apart so that each piece has a fan of leaves attached. Cut these back to good green leaves in a fan shape.

In the South, plant Bearded Iris at any time except immediately after bloom or in the dead of winter when the ground is subject to freezing. Plant them shallowly. Never cover the base of the leaves, and always expose the top of the rhizome where the leaves arise. Fertilize Iris plantings with a 6-12-12 or 5-10-15 formula in the early spring and again after they have finished blossoming.

The only serious pest of Bearded Iris is the Iris borer which starts in the leaves and works its way into the thick rhizome where it may be quite destructive. When the runs are first seen in the leaves, the plant should be sprayed with a systemic insecticide. When Iris are lifted and separated, the rhizome should be carefully examined for borers. If the rhizome is infested, carefully cut away the part in which the borer is found and treat the cut with dusting sulfur to prevent rot from starting.

Plant Dutch Iris bulbs in garden beds which have been prepared well and have excellent drainage. They grow and blossom best in full sun. Plant them about two inches deep and in groups, with the bulbs six inches apart. They prefer a pH above 6.5, so it is generally advisable to add limestone.

Japanese and Siberian Iris need the same kind of soil though their pH requirements are not so strict. They will take more shade than the Bearded or Dutch Iris. Plant them when they are not actively growing, usually in the fall or early spring.

LILIES
Lilium sp.

Bulb-forming Perennials
Summer flowering

There is nothing more spectacular in a garden than gorgeous Lilies in bloom. Unfortunately, most of the huge spectacular hybrid Lilies do not take to our heat and long growing season.

The easiest-to-grow Lily for us is the **Madonna Lily**, *L. candidum,* which has been a garden favorite for over 1,000 years.

Plant Lilies in a well-drained, well-prepared sunny spot to which liberal amounts of humus have been added. They need moisture when dry but cannot stand wet feet for any length of time. Fertilize them in the spring with a 6-12-12 or 5-10-15 formula.

The large fragrant white blossoms appear in June on five- to six-foot plants.

Plant Madonna Lilies in the early fall so that foliage may form before cold weather. Plant them with the top of the bulb only about an inch deep, since they are one of the stem-rooting Lilies.

NARCISSUS, including Daffodils, Jonquils, and others
Narcissus sp.

Bulb-forming Perennial
Spring flowering

Despite the fact that all Daffodils are Narcissus but not all Narcissus are Daffodils, there is a great deal of confusion about what is what. Nonetheless they are all suited to the South, and are one of our best sources of spring color.

The favorites have always been the large Trumpet Narcissus, which I have grown up calling Daffodil, and the little sweet-smelling, butter-yellow Jonquil (Johnny-Quil in much of the countryside). These two have the persistence of cast iron, and if properly planted, will last for years and years. My mother had a natural area of **King Alfred Daffodils** which has existed without disturbing for over thirty years.

There are other Narcissus that will last just as long when happy. My father once grew Narcissus bulbs commercially. Out in the field in front of his house are the remnants still of old plantings of **Laurens Koster** which have multiplied over the years into a several-acre mass, without any attention whatsoever.

In fact, there are few Narcissus that will not last for many years in a good planting. The choice of colors and types is almost infinite and one recommends cultivars merely by experience and taste, for almost all of them do well.

Choose an area with good drainage and prepare the soil deeply and well. Plant the bulbs, nose up, using the rule of thumb, i.e., the depth of planting three times the greatest diameter of the bulb. Narcissus do best in sun or part shade, but may be naturalized under deciduous trees which will let the sun through during the major growth period.

Narcissus need little care because they have very few problems. Fertilize with a 6-12-12 or 5-10-15 formula immediately after the blooms have faded. Do not remove the foliage until it turns yellow; if you do, you will ruin your plantings.

You do not need to lift and separate them until the flowers begin to diminish in size and most of the clump stops blossoming. If you need to do it, dig the clumps after the foliage has begun to die, separate the bulbs, and store in a cool dry place until late fall when you can reset the largest ones.

Plant Narcissus in November and December in most of the South, after the ground is cool. Earlier planting may cause the foliage to come up very early and be subject to damage in the winter from extreme cold.

I vote for the Narcissus as our most satisfactory bulb and one of the best of all our flowers.

❦ PEONY
Paeonia lactiflora and Hybrids

Tuberous-rooted Perennial
Spring flowering

I have a great love for Peonies. Their marvelous spring blossoms exceed those of any perennial plant I know. That is the good news. The bad news is that the South is not Peony country. However, this is one of the few plants which I truly believe is worth the time and effort to grow, even out of its favorite habitat.

You will never have Peonies like the ones in Oregon or even New England, but you can have Peonies which will bloom and give your garden that extra special character which only this plant can. But you must grow them under the

King Alfred Daffodil

Mass planting of King Alfred Daffodils

Festiva Maxima peony

Deep pink peony at Floweracres

A naturalized field of Laurens Koster Narcissus

Poeticus Narcissus

absolute best conditions, even altering their environment somewhat. It takes a combination of the right varieties, the right exposure, liming the soil to raise the pH, planting at the right depth, and controlling Botrytis in the spring. But it can be done, and it is not that hard.

The best way to start is by buying the old variety **Festiva Maxima**, which is a large double white with flecks of scarlet on some petals. It is tough and will perform here very well. There are other older varieties such as the pink, **Edulis Superba**, which will also perform well, but you should start with 'Festiva Maxima.'

Find a well-drained spot which gets full morning sun but shade from mid-afternoon on. Dig the bed deeply and add humus and perlite to give good drainage. Lime the bed to raise the pH above 6.5.

Purchase and plant Peony roots in the late fall. Look at the roots and choose only those with three or more bright pink buds showing. Plant them shallowly, ignoring the instructions that are usually attached or that you read in general publications, to plant them with the buds two inches deep. Since the bright pink buds need to freeze in the winter, they should be right at ground level and not buried.

Mulch the bed with pinestraw after planting but do not put the mulch over the buds. In the spring, fertilize with a 5-10-15 formula as the buds begin to sprout. At the same time, spray the buds and new shoots with Captan to control Botrytis. Spray again as the buds first begin to open.

Keep the bed well-mulched during the entire growing season and watered when the weather is dry. After the first winter, you will not have to mulch the bed until spring. Removing the old mulch in the late fall when the dead tops are removed will reduce the incidence of Botrytis.

The herbaceous Peonies, *P. lactifolia Hybrids*, are the only ones that I have ever had luck with in the South. **Tree Peonies** and **Japanese Peonies** (usually the singles) do not seem to do as well.

After you have mastered the art of Peony-growing with 'Festiva Maxima' and 'Edulis Superba,' you will want to branch out with other colors and forms. Be careful; not all will do well. Depend on the older mainstream varieties for your plantings and add a few of the "thriller" varieties as tests to see how they do.

❦ SPIDER LILY or RESURRECTION LILY
❦ *Lycoris* sp.

Bulb-forming Perennial
Late summer and fall flowering

The Spider Lilies have long been favorites in the South. They are often referred to as Resurrection Lilies because the foliage dies down, and then the flower stalk appears out of the ground rather suddenly in late summer. The pink flowers are an interesting study when they arise on a solitary stalk with no foliage to indicate that anything is underneath.

The *Lycoris squamigera* has heavier, more Lily-like flowers and is the more common one in the South. It will last for many, many years without lifting and resetting. One clump in our neighborhood is over 15 years old.

The *Lycoris radiata* is less persistent in the South but well worth planting for its unusual spidery flowers. The flowers are commonly red, though there is a white cultivar also available.

Plant Lycoris in the fall or early spring in drained and well-prepared soil where they may be left undisturbed for years. Plant *L. radiata* about five inches and *L. squamigera* about six inches deep. Apply a 6-12-12 or 5-10-15 fertilizer each spring as the leaves appear.

TUBEROSE
Polianthes tuberosa

Tuber-forming Perennial
Summer and fall flowering

Tuberoses are favorite plants of the Southern garden because of their summer and early fall flowering habits and wonderful fragrance. They should be set out in the spring after the ground begins to warm and the danger of frost has passed. The waxy white flowers appear in the mid to late summer, depending on how early they can be planted in a particular section of the South, and they bloom until fall.

Plant Tuberoses in a sunny, warm bed which has been well prepared and which has no drainage problems. Cover the tubers with about one inch of fine soil and fertilize with a standard 5-10-15 fertilizer.

The Tuberose can not stand a hard freeze touching the tuber. They must be mulched in the lower South where the ground may freeze lightly or lifted each fall, like Dahlias, and stored during the winter in the same manner as Caladiums.

TULIP
Tulipa sp.

Bulb-forming Perennial
Spring flowering

Tulips are beautiful and much prized, but they are not as happy here in our long growing seasons and warm springs as the Narcissus are. The best way to look at growing Tulips is as annuals, or at best, as three-year plants. A planting seldom lasts over three years except in the case of a few of the rock garden types.

The beauty of Tulips, however, makes their use worthwhile even as an annual, for few of our spring-flowering plants offer so much uniform color. There is nothing quite like a beautiful Tulip bed. There are hundreds of cultivars divided into several different classes, but most of us choose them by height, color, and blooming time.

Grow them in well-prepared beds that have good drainage and plenty of sun if you are going to keep them over several years. As annuals, they will bloom well in most well-drained locations.

Purchase Tulip bulbs early and store them in the refrigerator to prevent the damage to the flower bud inside the bulb which comes from too much warmth in most stores. The best planting time is November to December.

Lycoris radiata, Resurrection Lily

Tuberose

Lycoris squamigera

Red and yellow single tulips

Mass planting of tulips

Tulips will last longer if they are planted at least eight inches deep. Ignore the rule of thumb and instructions found in most books and on planting guides with the package. These are written for areas farther north, and they do not take into consideration our long, hot summers which cause the bulbs to split and form many small bulblets. This causes a deterioration of the flower size and reduces the effectiveness of the bulb.

There are many different types of Tulips from which to choose. These types vary in stem length, flower size and formation, bulb size, and blossoming time. In general, however, Tulips planted in the South will not have the variation in blossoming time as when planted in other parts of the country. There are a few very early types, usually the short-stem rock garden types like **Red Emperor**, which will blossom when the ground first warms in March. Almost all others will blossom in April or at latest in early May. It is difficult to classify Tulips in an orderly, useful way for us here. However, the following should help you choose the right ones for your garden.

TULIPS FOR THE SOUTH

BORDERS AND ROCK GARDENS	BEDDING AND CUT FLOWERS
(Usually last for many years)	*(Used as annuals for a few years)*
Kaufmanniana	Cottage *(Single or Double Flower)*
Fosterana	Darwin *(Single or Double Flower)*
Greigii	Fringed *(Single or Double Flower)*
	Parrot *(Lily Flower)*
	Triumph *(Lily Flower)*

Other Bulbous-Type Plants

The plants described above make up the more commonly used plants which are grown from underground storage organs. However, there are many others listed in catalogs and available in garden supply stores. There are a few that can be easily grown in the South and that are worth mentioning in abbreviated form.

Red Emperor tulip

OTHER BULBS FOR THE SOUTH

COMMON NAME AND BOTANICAL NAME	TYPE	HEIGHT	BLOSSOM TIME	EXPOSURE	PLANTING TIME	PLANTING DEPTH	FLOWERS
BLOOD LILY Haemanthus sp.	Bulb	18 in.	Late summer	Sun to light shade	Spring	5 in.	Large red balls
CALLA LILY Zantedeschia aethiopica	Rhizome	30 in.	Summer	Sun	Fall or early spring	8 in.	Unusual white spathe
COLCHICUM Colchicum sp.	Corm	5 to 8 in.	Usually fall	Sun	Fall or spring	2–4 in.	Various colors
CRINUM Crinum bulbispermum	Bulb	3 ft.	Late summer	Sun or light shade	Fall	5 in.	Lily-like, white and rose
GLORY-OF-THE-SNOW Chionodoxa Luciliae	Bulb	6 in.	Spring	Sun	Fall	5 in.	White, blue, pink
RAIN or FAIRY LILY Zephyranthes sp.	Bulb	6 in.	Late summer	Part to full sun	Fall or spring	2 in.	White or pink
SCILLA Scilla siberica	Bulb	6 in.	Early spring	Sun or part shade	Early spring	3 to 4 in.	Blue
SNOWDROP Galanthus nivalis	Bulb	6 to 10 in.	Early spring	Part sun	Fall	4 in.	White with green markings
SNOWFLAKE Leucojum aestivum	Bulb	6 in.	Early spring	Part sun	Fall	3 in.	Nodding white with green

Yellow Calla Lily

Crinum, Milk, and Wine Lily

Ginger Lily

Haemanthus, Blood-Lily

FORCING BULBS FOR OFF-SEASON BLOOM

When the winter is still dreary and spring seems years away, there is something you can do to bring spring flowers inside the house. This is to force bulbs for winter bloom.

Not all bulbs will force well and only a few are relatively foolproof. I have, for many years, made it a practice of forcing Paperwhite Narcissus for winter blossoms, especially for Christmas. In fact, one of the more appreciated Christmas gifts which Betsy and I have given over the years is a pot of Paperwhites just ready to bloom.

There are other bulbs which force easily, also. The giant South African Amaryllis is one of the easiest of all. These are the huge flowering bulbs which are so common at Christmas time.

Tulips, Crocus and Dutch Hyacinths may be forced also, but they require cold treatment which can become a real bother. I recommend that you stick with the easy ones, Paperwhites and Giant Amaryllis, so that results are insured and timing may be planned with certainty.

Paperwhite Narcissus forced for
winter bloom

Paperwhites showing extensive root
development

FORCING PAPERWHITE NARCISSUS

Be sure to buy a good strain of these bulbs. For some reason a few of the
strains do not have the sweet fragrance of others but rather a "spicy" odor
which to me is not that pleasant. I have found that the strain grown in
Southern France has the nicest odor and excellent forcing potential.

I force my Paperwhites in gravel and water since any effort to carry
them over after bloom is a useless trial. Remember, these bulbs are not
hardy like King Alfred and will not grow outside when the ground freezes
down to the bulb. Consider these as a one-time planting experience,
chucking them when the blossoms are spent and waiting until next time or
next year to start new bulbs.

The container may be any type that will hold water and will accom-
modate the number of bulbs you wish to force. I have found that a minimum of three bulbs are required to have a good planting. Fill the container
part way with clean gravel, marbles or any other coarse material which
will anchor the roots and hold the bulbs upright.

Press the bulbs into the planting material so that each one remains
upright. Now fill the bowl with more of the gravel or other material until
the bulbs are about two-thirds covered and well anchored. Some experts
recommend covering the bulbs only halfway, but I have found that there
is a tendency for the bulbs to push upward as the roots press downward
and topple over if less than two-thirds is covered.

Fill the bowl with water to the top of the gravel or other material,
wetting it thoroughly. Now carefully pour out water until that which remains is right under the bottom (basal plate) of the bulb. As the roots
develop, do not continue to add water until the roots have grown outward
and downward seeking the moisture. Then water sparingly without filling

up to the original level. This will cause the roots to search downward and keep the bulb in place rather than heaving upward.

Place the bowl in a bright spot but not in direct sunlight until the bloom buds appear. When you see the bloom buds breaking open, the plant may be placed wherever you like in the house.

Forcing time for the Paperwhite Narcissus will vary according to the temperature in your house, especially at night. On the average it will take from four to five weeks from planting until blossoms appear.

FORCING GIANT AMARYLLIS

The giant Amaryllis also force very easily and are prized as a flowering bulbous plant for Christmas and dreary winter times. Their monstrous flowers are set on tall, heavy stalks before the leaves appear. There are usually three huge blooms on each stalk.

Many garden shops sell these in a pre-planted pot which requires only the addition of water to force growth and the flower. However, you may also purchase individual bulbs from garden shops and mail order houses. These bulbs should be potted in a loose, peat-lite mixture in an eight-inch pot with the soil covering about one-quarter to one-half of the bulb. Merely water the soil thoroughly and growth will start almost immediately. It takes about six weeks for them to bloom, depending on the temperature of the house.

After the blossoms have finished, you will see the leaves appearing. Continue watering and fertilizing through the spring and summer. It is also wise to set the plant outside in a sunny spot during the summer but be sure it is kept watered and fertilized. In early September, stop watering and let the pot dry out. The leaves will turn yellow and become non-functional. Cut them off at the top of the bulb snout and place the pot in a dark cool spot. Leave it there until you are ready to force the bulb again.

Giant Amaryllis

Giant Amaryllis forced for Christmas bloom

CHAPTER 3

VINES FOR THE SOUTH

Porch swings and trellises were as much a part of the old days as almost anything else in the South. Before air conditioning sealed our houses, one of the coolest places to be was on the porch, protected from the sun by a wonderful vine. Rocking or swinging and talking to family, friends, and neighbors became a way of life. The porch was the summer living room for many of us. Everybody had a porch and every porch had a vine on a trellis or some other support. Now, vines seem to be only for mailboxes, lamp posts, and unsightly bird feeder poles.

Perhaps we have just forgotten about trellises. Decks or patios with a tendency to be hot as blazes can be cool and pleasant with a structure on which a vine can be grown to block the sun or give cooling shade. I spent four long, cold years at Cornell University, one of the "Ivy League" schools. The stone walls of the buildings are covered with ivy, Boston Ivy, that is. As a result, I have a tremendous feeling not only for vines used as cooling plants, but also for vines used to give beauty to structures in a way that no other plants can give.

The use of vines can express the personality of the gardener creatively. One fine gardener I know grew grape vines over her garage doors; another became a Clematis enthusiast and had white fences built around her entire garden area just to grow her dozens of different Clematis cultivars. I grew up with a Wisteria-covered arbor in the garden. Perhaps you have had a past experience with a vine that means as much to you as wild muscadine vines meant to me. We would cut and swing over the creek on these vines.

With a little imagination, there is almost no limit to how you can turn a humdrum garden and landscape into something exciting with the use of vines. One well-grown Clematis on a mailbox or bird feeder post can create as much interest as many beds of Azaleas.

Vines are interesting as well as beautiful. They can be trained to do many different landscape chores besides just adding beauty. They can

Luffa Gourd growing on a jungle gym

Clematis trained onto a birdfeeder pole

English Ivy covering
a wall

Poison Ivy is to be avoided.

Kudzu was imported to save the soil but destructively covers almost anything including trees.

provide shade when covering an arbor or trellis; they can cover up unsightly structures like concrete block walls, foundations, and ugly posts; they can be grown to block a view or restrict dust and noise.

Let your imagination run wild with vines and dare to be different! Don't be locked into what everybody else does. Try new and different ones in your creative projects.

Vines are also interesting plants to watch. Many grow tremendously each year; some, like the Sweet Autumn Clematis, have been reported to grow fifteen feet in a season.

Not all vines are useful; in fact, some are extraordinarily destructive. Kudzu, which was brought to us from the Orient to save our eroded land, has now become a serious pest. It outgrows the Clematis I mentioned by two or even three times. There is also Poison Ivy, *Rhus radicans*, which has caused immeasurable discomfort to so many, including my wife Betsy. "Leaves three, leave it be" is a good admonition to follow when working in the woods. Then there is our ever-present vine pest, Hall's Honeysuckle, *Lonicera japonica* cv. 'Halliana'. This has naturalized over much of our woodland area and can invade shrubs, trees, and almost anything in sight. Wild muscadine and naturalized Wisteria can wrap the trunk of a tree and strangle it. English Ivy growing on a pine may cause serious problems by either strangling as it wraps or by loosening and softening the bark, allowing pests to invade the tree trunk.

There are other interesting features of vines, such as how they climb. Some, like our beautiful native Carolina Jessamine, climb by twining around anything small enough to wrap. Others, like English Ivy, have rootlike discs which cling to a surface. Finally, there are vines like the grape whose tendrils reach out and wrap around a branch to hold up the main stem of the plant.

Carolina Jessamine climbs by twining.

Wild Honeysuckle will ruin a forest if left unchecked.

English Ivy climbs by attaching its discs to a wall.

ALL ABOUT VINES FOR THE SOUTH

I will be discussing vines in two groups: vines of a permanent nature like those that are woody and remain for years; and herbaceous vines, like those that either die to the ground each year and return the next from the crown, or that are annual and last for just one season.

Woody Vines

The permanent woody vines make up the preponderance of our plantings. Some are evergreen, many flower, and all those I discuss will last for many years. Choose the type carefully, plant it properly, train it well, and you will have much to enjoy. The following are the best for the South:

CAROLINA JESSAMINE
Gelsemium sempervirens

Climbing Method: Twining
Vigor: Excellent
Exposure: Full sun to moderate shade
Foliage: Semi-evergreen
Blossoms: Yellow, aromatic
Pruning Time: After bloom
Time of Bloom: Late spring
Problems: All plant parts contain gelsemine, a poison which can cause sickness to humans and animals when ingested

The native Carolina Jessamine vine is one of the toughest plants, thriving on abuse and growing vigorously and rapidly. Though it needs loose, high-humus soil really to excel, it will grow in most soils.

The blossoms are yellow, aromatic, and profuse.

LARGE FLOWERING CLEMATIS
Clematis X

Climbing Method: Tendrils
Vigor: Poor to moderate (good soil prevails)
Exposure: Morning sun
Foliage: Deciduous
Blossoms: Large; various colors
Pruning Time: Winter, except as noted
Time of Bloom: Spring and summer
Problems: Must be grown properly or will not grow well

The giant hybrid Clematis are some of the most beautiful flowers you will find in a garden. The heavy vines will cover a post, trellis, or fence and provide an unsurpassed show of flowers.

Carolina Jessamine

Sweet Autumn Clematis

Clematis, 'Lanuginosa candida'

Clematis, 'Ramona'

These hybrids, however, are not the easiest of plants to grow. In our hot summers, they do suffer unless they are given proper growing conditions. If they are planted and forgotten, the results will be terribly disappointing.

The old adage "Plant a dollar plant in a ten dollar hole" is perhaps truer of Clematis than of any other plant grown. They must have rich, well-drained, non-acid soil. The pH should be above 6.2, which means that most of our soil should be regularly limed or the plants fertilized yearly with bone meal.

Choose a location which is protected from the hot afternoon sun but which receives four or more hours of full sun each day.

Dig a very large hole, two feet wide and two to three feet deep. If your soil is very tight and sticky and drains poorly, place six inches of coarse gravel or pine bark chunks in the bottom of the hole. Mix equal proportions of peat moss, perlite, ground bark, and soil together to refill the hole. Add a large double handful of bone meal to the mixture. If there are dogs in the area which might be attracted to the bone meal, use ground limestone.

Remove bare root plants from the package and determine the size of the roots. Refill the hole to the level of the bottom of the roots. Pull the soil mixture into the hole as you hold and spread the roots naturally. The top of the roots should be at the soil level when the hole is filled. Pack the soil around the roots, being careful not to leave any air pockets. Make a saucer of soil around the plant to hold water. Now water slowly and thoroughly, checking when finished to see if the top roots have been exposed as the soil settled. If so, cover them very lightly with the soil mixture. Do not cover the stem with soil.

Since the roots need to be cool at all times, a heavy mulch is wise. However, I discovered a variation on an English system my mother learned many years ago. The English drive a short terra cotta pipe into the ground around the Clematis when planting. My way is to chip out the bottom of an eight-inch clay pot. Invert the pot over the newly-planted Clematis and press into the ground a couple of inches, allowing the top of the plant to peek out of the inverted pot. Mulch with pine straw an area a couple of feet in diameter around the pot. This keeps away weeds and holds moisture evenly in the ground.

Clematis will grow for years with few problems if they are planted correctly at the first. They do need fertilizing at least once a year with a slow-release nitrogen fertilizer which is high in phosphate and potassium. Apply bone meal or limestone every spring to keep the soil sweet.

Pruning properly at the right time is necessary. When and how to prune is determined by the type of Clematis you purchase.

Insects do attack Clematis on occasion. Thrips are particularly bad on Duchess of Edinburgh and may be seen on *Henryi* and *Lanuginosa Candida*. Spray with a recommended thrip control. Japanese Beetles and the Clematis Blister Beetle will attack the foliage. Sevin will control both of these very well.

TYPES OF CLEMATIS

There are different types of Clematis, depending on which parents were used in hybridizing. The three major groups are (1) the *florida* group, (2) the *patens* group, and (3) the *Jackmanii* group. Most of the ones we grow are in the Jackmanii group. These blossom on the current season's growth and need heavy pruning in the winter. There are several common cultivars belonging to either the Florida or the Patens group which need very little pruning, and then only after blossoming has finished.

HYBRID CLEMATIS FOR THE SOUTH

JACKMANII GROUP
Prune heavily in winter

CULTIVAR	COLOR
Edo Muraski	clear blue
Hagley Hybrid	pink with purple anthers
Henryi*	white with yellow stamens
C. X Jackmanii	deep purple
Lanuginosa Candida*	white with darker stamens
Lord Neville	deep purple
Mrs. Cholmondalay	pure blue
M. Edouard Andre	rose red
Ramona*	purple-blue
Ville de Lyon	carmen-red
Will Goodwin	deep blue/frilled petal

FLORIDA AND PATENS GROUP
Prune lightly and sparingly, after bloom

CULTIVAR	COLOR
Duchess of Edinburgh	double white
Nelly Mosser*	pink with dark bars

Note: Cultivars marked * are particularly good in the South

🌿 SWEET AUTUMN CLEMATIS
Clematis paniculata (Clematis dioscoreifolia var. *robusta)*

Climbing Method: Twining
Vigor: Excellent
Exposure: Sun to part shade
Foliage: Deciduous
Blossoms: White, small, profuse, fragrant
Pruning Time: Winter
Time of Bloom: Late summer
Problems: Japanese Beetles and Clematis Beetles on occasion

Though this is one of the easiest of all Clematis to grow, many gardeners fail to see its potential because the flowers are individually small, unlike the huge hybrid flowers, and because the bloom time is concentrated over a short period in the late summer and early fall. What a pity, for this vine is spectacular and will cover a much wider area than any of the hybrids.

It is extremely easy to grow, not requiring the extensive soil preparation required by the hybrids. It will grow in any good garden soil and takes only yearly pruning and fertilizing.

CONFEDERATE JASMINE
Trachelospermum jasminoides

Climbing Method: Twining
Vigor: Moderate
Exposure: Light to moderate shade, protected from the cold west wind and Southern winter sun
Foliage: Evergreen
Blossoms: Waxy, white, star-shaped, and very fragrant
Pruning Time: Lightly, after bloom
Time of Bloom: Spring and early summer
Problems: May be damaged by cold

This is one of the really Southern plants in the class with Gardenia, Banana Shrub, and *Camellia Japonica*. On the coast and in other moderate areas in the winter, they are widely grown and loved, but they are questionable for most of the South except in protected areas. The flowers have a rich fragrance, and the foliage is evergreen.

The Confederate Jasmine is a plant we all want but may have some difficulty keeping when the temperature drops below ten degrees F. It should be given plenty of protection from the northwest winter winds and from the hot Southern sun when the ground is frozen.

Its rewards are great when it is grown in a spot or area where cold will not damage it.

Asiatic Jasmine, *Trachelospermum asiaticum*, is listed as being hardier, but I haven't found the difference that great. It also has a pale yellow blossom.

CREEPING FIG
Ficus pumila (formerly *Ficus repens*)

Climbing Method: Clinging
Vigor: Moderate in a protected place
Exposure: Part to full shade
Foliage: Evergreen
Blossoms: Insignificant
Pruning Time: Spring and early summer
Problems: Subject to cold damage

Purple Wisteria floribunda

Creeping Fig

English Ivy used with a garden statue

The Creeping Fig is a marvelous plant to cover shaded and protected walls. It has small leaves and lies flat against the surface. It grows in considerable shade and will cover walls in a much more refined fashion than English Ivy.

It is subject to cold damage when the temperature drops to about 10 degrees. However, heavy mulching will save the root system and the plant will rapidly recover and spread over the area once again. The only bother is having to remove the old dead vine from the wall, because it holds fast.

ENGLISH IVY
Hedera Helix

Climbing Method: Clinging
Vigor: Excellent
Exposure: Part sun to shade
Foliage: Evergreen
Blossoms: Insignificant
Pruning Time: Winter, spring, and summer
Problems: Rampant growth

English Ivy creeps and leaps over and through every area where it is happy. Given the right conditions, it will cover banks, walls, trees, and anything else which it can cling to or crawl over. It is rather coarse and may become a pest if not controlled. It is an excellent vine with few problems and, once established, it will do well all by itself. If anything, it is overused and often planted in poor soil and hot sun, where it looks ratty. In the shade, it will perform beautifully.

Establishing a bed of English Ivy is not difficult if you will start with plants and not runners. Small, well-rooted plants set on one- or two-foot centers in well-prepared soil will cover an area in a single year. As a climbing vine, set the plants two to three feet apart and attach the first runners to the structure. Fertilize the first couple of years with a slow-release nitrogen, complete formula evergreen fertilizer. After English Ivy is established, there will be little need, if any, for a maintenance fertilizer application.

Do not allow English Ivy to climb trees because the hold-fast rootlets will penetrate the bark and cause problems, especially on pines. It should never be allowed to climb wooden fences or other wood structures because the action of the rootlets along with the moisture held against the wood will cause rotting.

GOLDFLAME HONEYSUCKLE
Lonicera Heckrottii

Climbing Method: Slightly twining but needs supporting
Vigor: Moderate
Exposure: Sun to part shade
Foliage: Semi-evergreen
Blossoms: Clusters of tubular "honeysuckles," rose with yellow throats
Pruning Time: Winter

Time of Bloom: Heavy in early summer, light through the rest of the summer
Problems: Must be supported

The Goldflame Honeysuckle is the best of the Honeysuckles to use on mailboxes, posts, fences, or trellises because it does not become a pest like the wild one, which we seem to spend our lives fighting.

Since it blossoms on new shoots, do not prune it during the summer or the flowers will be reduced. It will need fertilizer in the spring to force the bloom growth.

SILVER FLEECEVINE
Polygonum Aubertii

Climbing Method: Twining
Vigor: Excellent
Exposure: Sun to light shade
Foliage: Deciduous
Blossoms: Racemes of white flowers
Pruning Time: Winter
Time of Bloom: Late summer
Problems: None to worry about

The Silver Fleecevine is not used nearly as much as it should be, for it blooms in late summer when few other vines and shrubs are blooming except Sweet Autumn Clematis. It is a rapid grower and blooms on the new shoots, so prune it heavily each winter.

Some consider this a suitable substitute for the Climbing Hydrangea, *Hydrangea anomala petiolaris*, which has not proved satisfactory in our climate. Actually, the Silver Fleecevine is quite different since the Climbing Hydrangea is a clinging vine and blossoms much earlier.

VIRGINIA CREEPER
Parthenocissus quinquefolia

Climbing Method: Tendrils with adhesive discs
Vigor: Excellent
Exposure: Part sun to shade
Foliage: Deciduous, turns bright red in the fall
Blossoms: Insignificant
Pruning Time: Winter primarily, but any time except late summer and fall
Problems: Foliage is rather loose and open

The native Virginia Creeper is too often overlooked because it is common in the woods. It will easily cover a shady wall and is less rank and thick than English Ivy. The latter is used much more because it is evergreen, a fact that has little meaning when everything else in the garden is dormant anyway.

There are some cultivars of Virginia Creeper with smaller leaves which give a thicker and more refined appearance.

The "Ivy" of my college walls, Boston Ivy, *Parthenocissus tricuspidata,* may also be used and is tighter and more refined. It is deciduous also, and thus is overlooked by most Southern gardeners.

WISTERIA
Wisteria sp.

Wisterias were used in the old South far more than they are now. Three problems with the plant have reduced its popularity. First, it is a rank grower and may climb trees and everything in sight unless kept under control. Second, there is often a problem in getting the numbers of showy blossoms desired. Third, it seeds freely and is likely to come up all over the place.

There are two types grown in gardens. The first, *Wisteria floribunda* (referred to as *W. multijuga* in the past) or Japanese Wisteria, has the longest racemes of flowers, but they do not open all at once. The second, *Wisteria sinensis* or Chinese Wisteria, has shorter racemes, but all the flowers open at once.

Both Wisterias may be encouraged to set more blossoms by root pruning in the early spring and by fertilizing with high phosphate fertilizers like 6-12-12 or pure Superphosphate. Pruning the elongated shoots after bloom in the early summer will encourage the bloom buds for the next season to set.

CHINESE WISTERIA
Wisteria sinensis

Climbing Method: Twining, left to right
Vigor: Extraordinary
Exposure: Sun to light shade
Foliage: Deciduous
Blossoms: Long racemes of purple or white flowers, all flowers in the cluster opening at once
Pruning Time: After bloom
Time of Bloom: Spring, usually before the Japanese Wisteria
Problems: Seeds freely and grows out of bounds easily

JAPANESE WISTERIA
Wisteria floribunda

Climbing Method: Twining, right to left
Vigor: Extraordinary
Exposure: Sun to light shade
Foliage: Deciduous
Blossoms: Very long racemes of purple or white, opening unevenly
Pruning Time: After bloom
Time of Bloom: Spring, after the Chinese Wisteria
Problems: Seeds freely, and grows out of bounds easily

Herbaceous Vines

There are many situations where a permanent woody vine is not suitable but where a climbing herbaceous annual or perennial vine would be an attractive addition to the garden. There are many of these vines which may be grown from seed and a few from tubers, rhizomes, or some other type of underground storage organ or, as the country people say, "from a potato."

One of the best gardening adventures I have had recently occurred after we returned from Egypt when we found that the beautiful Clematis on our bird feeder pole had passed away. Not having time to get a new Clematis started, I planted a few seeds of Heavenly Blue Morning Glory along with a few seeds of Moonflower. The combination of blue flowers by day and white flowers at night brought great joy to all. We would even make a habit of going into the garden to watch the white Moonflowers opening, a sight similar to watching time-lapse photography.

Here are a few good herbaceous vines to consider. Don't let this list be final, though. Try any you hear about that might suit your purposes.

❦ BLACK-EYED SUSAN VINE
Thunbergia alata

Perennial which may not come back

Black-Eyed Susan is a delightful heavy vine which is started from seed but may return each year from the old crown. The flowers are orange to gold with a black center and bloom all summer. Black-Eyed Susan Vine will cover a fence nicely and is excellent on ugly chain link fences which are difficult to hide.

❦ CLIMBING FERN
Lygodium palmatum

Perennial-like, with tops killed each winter

My mother called this a climbing Maidenhair Fern, not so much because it looks like a real Maidenhair, but because it is so graceful and finely foliaged. It thrives in damp places where little else will grow except English Ivy. I had one on my St. Francis bird feeder post for many years, and it thrived where little else would grow.

If you mulch the crown heavily after the top is killed by cold, it should return each year from the crown. I found to my chagrin that it is a mite tender at 0 degrees, and without mulch it may not return. Mine didn't. The spores are quite fertile, and it will "seed" freely. Take up a couple of the young plants and put them in a very protected place to have in case of another winter like 1983-84.

Climbing Fern will grow ten to twelve feet in a year and will be quite full all the way to the top.

Climbing Fern

Scarlet Runner bean

Luffa sponge gourd

Heavenly Blue Morning Glory on a bird feeder

❧ CYPRESS VINE
Ipomoea Quamoclit

Annual

Cypress Vine is a delightful climber with "Cypress-type" foliage and red tubular flowers during much of the summer. Grow it in the sun in rich, loose soil. Start the seed inside in a tray or in a greenhouse or hot bed. Plant in the garden as soon as the danger of frost has passed.

❧ MOONFLOWER
Ipomoea alba

Annual

This is a rapidly-growing vine with rather large foliage which is heavily set and covers the main stems and branches well. The large white flowers open in the late afternoon and evening. It will cover a ten-foot trellis or post in a few months and will be beautiful until frost each year.

❧ MORNING GLORY
Ipomoea nil (also *tricolor*)

Annual

The Morning Glory may be the scourge of the farmer's fields and my vegetable garden, but on a trellis, post, or fence, the cultivated forms are beautiful and should not be discriminated against. There are reds, whites, and blues, but the best of all, in my opinion, is the old Heavenly Blue.

Start them all from seed which has been soaked overnight in warm water or notched with a file to break the hard seed coat and encourage quick germination. Seed directly in the spot where the vines are to grow. Keep well-fertilized to force the growth and bloom.

❧ PASSION FLOWER
Passiflora incarnata

Annual

I do not understand why our common Maypop, Passion Flower, is not used as a vine in our gardens. I will never forget seeing them in Israel, where the beautiful flowers covered whole walls.

I list it with reservation since few seed companies have the seed. If you see a packet, buy it and try this lovely plant which is usually relegated to our ditch banks and open, unused fields.

SCARLET RUNNER BEAN
Phaseolus coccineus

Annual

Scarlet Runner is an old-time bean with numerous red bean flowers which will act much like any climbing bean, but with more colorful and ornamental flowers. The beans it produces are edible. Plant in loose, well-drained soil as soon as the ground begins to warm. Fertilize frequently to keep the flowers blooming. It will blossom until frost.

Other Vines to Use

The woody and herbaceous vines are those most commonly used in the garden. There are others which, as I mentioned in the beginning, may be used in a creative way to show the personality of the gardener. Any trailing vegetables whose fruits are not so heavy as to pull down the vine make interesting and decorative plants for fences, trellises, and arbors.

GRAPE
Vitis sp.

The common grape of the fruit garden may be used as an ornamental as well as a fruiting vine. The muscadine grape was grown for years on arbors under which older Southerners used to sit quite shaded from the hot summer sun. I have seen the common grape used on trellises and over finials on carports and garages.

GOURDS
Luffa, Cucurbita, Lagenaria, and others

Gourds, especially the ornamental and unusually-shaped types, are excellent vines for all sorts of garden situations. They will add a great deal of interest to any garden. The flowers of gourds, while not spectacular, are attractive, and of course the fruits are the conversation pieces. Some, like the Luffa, have very long runners and should be used on larger structures.

See Volume II on Vegetables for their culture.

POLE BEANS
Phaseolus vulgaris

The common Pole Bean is a useful ornamental as well as a wonderful plant of the vegetable garden. It is tough, tenacious, and will climb ten to fifteen feet very quickly after the weather warms in the spring. It makes an excellent plant for trellises and arbors as well as chain link fences.

For Pole Bean culture, see Volume II on Vegetables.

CHAPTER 4

HOUSEPLANTS FOR THE SOUTH

We all dream of surrounding ourselves with the natural beauty found in living, growing plants. That is why we become gardeners. The gardens we develop are really outdoor living areas where we can totally immerse ourselves in creative beauty and fulfill the almost universal desire to live with the beauty of natural things. Until modern technology provided a way to have uniform warmth throughout our homes and artificial light in great amounts, our gardens had to stay outside, growing at the mercy of the climate of the area in which we live.

In places like the tropics where the climate is warm all the time, it is easy to merge the sheltered life inside a home with the natural environment outside. There is no problem with freezing weather or drastic, seasonal changes which disrupt the growth pattern of plants. The plant lover has only to set a pot where the light conditions are acceptable and the garden moves inside.

However, in the temperate zone the situation is quite different. Inside buildings we create a comfortable but artificial environment to help us survive the low and sometimes freezing temperatures found during parts of each year. But before the engineers gave us bright electric lights and central heat, there was very little success in growing plants inside. Away from the fireplace, it was too

103

Growing plants inside means growing them away from their native habitats. Adjust the indoor environment to suit their needs. A well grown Dumb Cane.

Indoor plants make a home more liveable.

Homes in the tropics have plants merging between inside and outside with little effort. Macarthur Palm near a covered swimming pool in Kuala Lumpur

Betsy Hastings' orchids, Kuala Lumpur

In the tropics plants grow the entire year outside. A palm in Kuala Lumpur

In the tropics many people use jungle plants in pots as decoration for areas between inside and outside. A Bird's Nest Fern at the Merlin Hotel, Kuantan, Malaysia

cold for the types of plants which might possibly survive the low light intensity inside. In place of living and growing beauty, people used art to give themselves a feeling of the natural environment which they so deeply desired. Paintings of flowers or landscapes were the only way that most homeowners were able to have the feeling of living in a natural setting when the weather outside was intolerable.

A few of the most wealthy built a glasshouse nearby, from which they could bring a beautiful potted plant or a bouquet of hothouse flowers for a quick stay in the often miserably cold house.

When technology brought us an efficient method of keeping homes uniformly warm in the winter, we immediately began searching for suitable plants to grow inside. Finding these plants has not been easy. No plant is native to the inside of a house; or, to put it conversely, every plant we try to grow inside has been introduced from a different, less hostile environment. These two facts together are the crux of the difficulties in growing plants inside our homes.

The ground under Oil Palm trees is covered with mushrooms showing the very high humidity normal in the tropical forests.

Most of our house plants have been brought from an equatorial and tropical environment. Tropical plants grow year round because the native temperature, daylight hours, and growing conditions are almost even throughout the year. Therefore, they do not need a dormant period to initiate a new cycle of growth.

The artificially-produced year-round environment of a heated and air-conditioned house would seem to be perfect for these plants which know no seasons in their native habitats. The problem encountered, however, is lack of humidity. The tropical jungle is very humid, while our homes are dry as a desert.

At a given temperature, the body feels more comfortable the lower the humidity. My work in the Sahara Desert in Egypt and in the jungles of Southeast Asia has introduced me poignantly to this problem. I struggled to stay comfortable in the Philippines and Malaysia at cooler temperatures than I found in the desert in Egypt. Sweat pours off as I work today in Malaysia, while in the shade in Egypt I was relatively comfortable at much higher temperatures. The engineers have designed home and office heating systems to provide people with the driest, most comfortable environment possible. Unfortunately, what makes us most comfortable is hardest on plants which are native to the jungle.

Another serious difficulty for plants growing inside is light intensity. Houses are not brightly lighted inside. Though electric lights have helped, the light intensity found in most homes is very low indeed compared to light conditions outside, even in shady areas.

The best plants for inside the home are tropical plants of the jungle floor or inhabitants of jungle trees which thrive in low light areas. I have been in jungles which seemed dark and scary, yet the amount of light the plants actually get there may be greater than in a brightly lit house.

Another group of plants which might seem to fit the environment of the home comes from the deserts which know little change from season to season. Though many of these plants do quite well, some suffer greatly because of insufficient light. Desert plants grow where there is almost no shade. Unless we provide special effort and many lights, we cannot equal the desert environment of high light intensity inside a home.

Plants of the jungle floor often make excellent plants for indoors due to lower light requirements.

Ferns in the tops of jungle trees get more light than you would expect.

Plants of the desert need lower humidity but more light than most houses have.

Air conditioning dries the air to such a degree that plants suffer. Burning of the edges and tips of the leaves of many plants results from too low humidity.

Air conditioning is almost as disastrous for plants as central heating because it dries the atmosphere even more. Tropical plants really suffer more in a summer of air conditioning than in a winter of artificial heating.

The art of growing plants inside the house becomes a balancing act between human needs and plant needs. Humans are more comfortable when the humidity is low; tropical plants do best when it is high. And low-humidity plants from the desert need high light intensity, which the nature of most buildings prevents. Gardening inside becomes a horticultural task requiring different practices from those we use growing plants in our gardens outside. But it is a gardening adventure with great rewards for those who feel the need to live with plants each day of the year, both outside in their gardens and inside their homes.

PLANTS FROM THE TROPICS

The view from our sixth floor apartment in Alexandria, Egypt, included The Admiral's Garden below us. Weeping Fig, *Ficus nitida*, formed the hedge; Elephant Ear Caladiums, *Colocasia esculenta*, abounded; beautiful Hibiscus, *Hibiscus Rosa-sinensis*, were everywhere; and there were two huge palms rising from the garden.

This was my first introduction to a land which saw no freezing temperatures and where the "tropical" plants I had tried to grow inside our home in Sweet Apple were growing easily and naturally. This was nothing, however, like my first view of the real tropics when I arrived in the Philippines. Rizal Park, across from the hotel, was filled with plants from books I had read or plants which I had never seen except in a pot or tub. Frangipani, *Plumeria rubra*, were everywhere; Coconut Palms, *Cocos nucifera*, arched upward; Elephant Ears, *Colocasia sp.* and *Alocasia sp.*, which we seldom if ever see, were growing from every damp spot. The trip to Baguio looking

Anthurium beside a road in the Philippines

Frangipani is a wonderful tree of the tropics with sweet smelling blossoms.

Orchids are easily grown in tropical gardens.

Colocasias (Elephant Ears) abound in the tropics. The roots are used as a nutritious food called Taro, which is eaten in place of potatoes.

Tropical countries abound in unusual plants like this tree fern in Manila.

A huge Bougainvillea grown as a shrub on Mindanao, Philippines

Spathyphyllum growing in the Philippines

Kapok, used in the finest pillows, grows naturally on the Island of Guimaras, Philippines.

Unusual miniature Caladiums found growing at a Barrio home in the Philippines.

Ruby, a Filipina friend, with her orchid, which grows happily outside in the warm climate of the Island of Guimaras, Philippines

for cool farmland was one of the most exciting trips I have ever taken. Growing wild beside the road was a new world of plant materials. I could not believe the seemingly infinite forms of Elephant Ears, the size of the trees, and the multitude of blooming plants which were new to me.

Every day brought more horticultural discoveries. I flew to Laguna, then to Mindanao, then to Panay. Orchids, seen before only in corsages, were common in the simplest gardens; wild plants like mahogany trees, Caladiums, and cashews grew beside the roads; huge banana and pineapple estates adjoined the sugar plantations for which Mindanao is famous. The islands of Panay and Guimaras introduced me to mangoes, cocoa, kapok, jackfruit, breadfruit, miniature Caladiums, Acacia, and a myriad of Hibiscus and Bougainvillea.

Jackfruit on Guimaras, Philippines

Philodendron growing on a tree in Green Park, Makati, Manila

Our well-known Dumb Cane, Dieffenbachia, in a mass planting in Manila

My year in the Philippines was an eye opener. Reverting to the stateside nurseryman that I once was, I constantly thought how much a plant I saw growing wild would bring at home in a nursery container.

Unfortunately, U.S. colonialism and Marcos cronyism in the Philippines has wiped out much of the primeval jungle there. In Malaysia, by contrast, British colonialism and more enlightened self-government has preserved huge amounts of the primordial state of nature. The road to the famous Cameron Highlands cuts through some of the most beautiful forests I have ever seen. Huge trees form canopies over twenty-foot-high tree ferns. It is like a tropical botanical garden which goes on and on for dozens of miles. Malaysia is a land of huge jungles and immense plantings of oil palm and rubber trees. To my surprise, these were not the rubber plants, *Ficus elastica,* of our homes, but a smaller-leafed plant, *Hevea brasiliensis,* with a very different growth habit.

A beautiful double hibiscus being admired by a young Filipino on Guimaras

Breadfruit growing on Guimaras, Philippines

Palms lining the campus avenues of the University of the Philippines, Los Banos

A tree fern on the road to the Cameron Highlands, Malaysia

Tapping a rubber tree

Commercial rubber tree

My insight into the world of tropical plants, however, matured when I became involved in developing a 2,500-acre vegetable farm in former jungle land, and my family and I moved to Kuala Lumpur, Malaysia.

Luckily my first trip to our project site was with Datuk Ibrahim bin Ismail, general manager of the Development Authority of Pahang-Tenggara, and his very able assistant George Tee. George, a trained ecologist who obtained his Master of Business Administration degree in England, introduced me to the jungle. There I discovered many of our tropical house plants growing in nature, each with an explanation by George as to why they did well in the house or yard.

This palm was found growing in the jungle left on our farm in Malaysia.

We saved this huge Staghorn fern from the bulldozer, and it is still thriving in the top of a tree on our farm in Malaysia.

John Huyck rescued this friend, a Bird's Nest fern, from a tree on our farm.

Oil Palms are a huge commercial crop in Malaysia.

Now these plants became friends of mine in their natural setting. When trees were felled, we rescued giant tree ferns and potted them to decorate the office or apartment. We moaned when a Staghorn Fern perished as the jungle was cleared.

In Kuala Lumpur, the yard of our house was filled with some of the most beautiful plants of all. There were Sealing Wax Palms, *Cyrtostachys Lakka,* with their bright red trunks; single and double Hibiscus, *H. Rosa-sinensis;* Ixora, *I. coccinea;* Cigar Flower, *Cuphea ignea;* Red Ginger Plant, *Alpinia purpurata,* Bird's-nest Fern, *Asplenium nidus;* several single- and double-flowered Bougainvillea, mangoes, rambutan, guava, and palms which I was never able to identify exactly. The environment so intrigued us that Betsy developed a collection of beautiful orchids.

Suddenly, tropical plants became a part of my gardening life there just as Azaleas and Camellias are in Sweet Apple. Happily, I learned how

Double Bougainvillea

Bougainvilleas come in many colors and forms.

This Sealing Wax Palm was growing in the garden in Kuala Lumpur, Malaysia.

115

Ixora, a good inside-outside flowering plant

A spectacular double red Hibiscus in the author's garden, Kuala Lumpur.

One of Betsy Hastings' orchids in Kuala Lumpur, Malaysia

Red Ginger, a wonderful plant for gardens in the tropics and for inside or outside in the South

The hibiscus is grown in the tropics like we grow roses in the southern United States. They make excellent inside-outside plants in the South.

The entrance to the author's home in Kuala Lumpur, with familiar plants which are grown inside in the southern United States

to grow them naturally, which helps bring better success when growing them in a pot at home in the southern United States.

Living near tropical jungles and working to develop a farm on land once covered by huge primordial forests has given me a different perspective for growing these plants in and around my home in Sweet Apple.

Jungle soil is extremely different from what you would expect. It is beautiful for growing plants! The tilth is loose and the long years of natural growth have produced some of the best growing media imaginable. After a 3-inch rainfall, our former jungle has had neither puddles nor washing; the drainage is fantastic. The soil is also very fertile because of the hundreds, perhaps thousands, of years of natural organics which have been added from decaying plants.

I have carefully watched plants which were removed from this environment, potted, and taken to our house. Too often, they grow as poorly. Incredibly, drainage is most often the culprit. It would seem that plants from the tropics with huge amounts of rain would need tremendous amounts of water. Yet, in the tropical jungle, the soil is so loose and porous that there is seldom too much water, while in a pot in Kuala Lumpur or in Sweet Apple, overwatering is a definite problem.

Another factor in the jungle is the heavy air. I am sure at some time you have been inside a greenhouse when the temperature was near 100 degrees. Remember how uncomfortable it was? That feeling is much like being in a jungle day and night. It seems you could squeeze water out of

A field of Sweet Corn at the author's project in Malaysia. This land was jungle one year prior to this picture.

Monkey in a tree near our farm—a typical jungle inhabitant

Jungle soil is loose and porous, not heavy like some so-called jungle mixes which you buy in stores.

the air if you tried. The reason for the discomfort is not only the high heat, but more importantly, the high humidity.

In fact, the jungle is an unpleasant place for most humans. All of us "orang orang putih" ("white men" to the Malaysians) suffer greatly from the heat, humidity, and insects, not to mention white-eyed cobras, pythons, wild boars, and a loose tiger or two.

Jungles are hot, humid, and inhabited by monkeys and other animals.

Python caught by a catcher who sells the hides and meat

A huge tree of the jungle

You might spot a lazy iguana in a jungle tree.

This is the environment from which many houseplants have been taken. To make them do their best, you would have to duplicate this forbidding jungle environment, which no one in his right mind would want to do. Instead, you must concentrate your indoor gardening efforts on helping these tropical plants adapt to an environment inside your home, which is more comfortable for us and distinctly less inviting for them.

Many books on houseplants go into more detail than space permits me here. But their approach is generally from the standpoint of a nursery-grown plant being taken into the home, with little regard for where that plant or its ancestors actually came from. My approach is to tell you how to help plants which I have seen growing in their natural environment adapt to an indoor environment which is strange to them, and how to keep them growing well with good gardening practices, rather than just give you "tricks of the trade" and individual plant recommendations. When we have finished this chapter, I hope you will understand better how to handle your plants in their new and rather hostile environment.

THE ESSENTIALS FOR GROWTH

All plants must have certain things to grow well. In previous volumes of this series I have explained the basic needs of plants in a garden environment, but not in the environment of a house or building. The essentials, though, are the same: light (including the length of the day and night hours), heat (temperature), water (including humidity), nutrients, a suitable medium in which to grow, and protection from insects and diseases.

Though house plants have the same basic requirements, the gardener must remember at all times that these plants are not in their natural environment. They have been taken suddenly from a most cooperative growing area to one which is less cooperative, even hostile.

The following inhibiting conditions must constantly be reckoned with in indoor gardening:
- The low light intensity of many rooms in our homes
- The low humidity when the furnace or air conditioner is operating
- The size of the container holding the plant, which is very small compared with the growing area of the plant in its natural state
- The variable number of light and dark hours in our seasons, compared with the almost even number of light and dark hours in the tropics.

Furthermore, growing plants successfully indoors involves attention to:
- Providing a better environment than that normally found inside modern buildings
- Choosing the best plants for any set of conditions indoors
- Adapting outside growing practices to fit the restricted soil area provided by pots or planters
- Altering set practices during the transition periods in spring, when the heat is turned off and the air conditioning is turned on, and in the fall, when the air conditioning is turned off and the heat is turned on.

THE BEST ENVIRONMENT

The first essential to provide for indoor plants is higher humidity. Most of the year the air in our homes and buildings is very dry. Lately it has been

Low humidity can be harmful to tropical plants. Note the dying back of the tips of this fan palm.

suggested that this dry air is not as healthy for us as we previously thought; many doctors now recommend humidifying the air which passes through the central heating system. This helps plants to a certain degree, but even the humidifier on a furnace does not raise the relative humidity in a building as high as it was in the native habitats of most house plants. One of the best helps I have found is a simple cold-air vaporizer. If you will place one of these vaporizers among groups of house plants, you will be surprised how quickly their growth improves.

There are other satisfactory methods of raising the humidity. Spraying the plant's foliage with a fine mist of fresh water once or twice a day will help, especially during the transition periods from heating to air-conditioning. When you set pots in groups, try placing them on gravel in a watertight pan. Fill the pan with water about halfway up the gravel. Do not allow the pots, however, to sit in water.

Do not place plants near an open heat vent or in the stream of air from an air conditioner. The drying effect from either source will make your plants suffer badly.

The second essential to provide for indoor plants is more light. Try taking your camera into a shady area outdoors which you think is similar to the light conditions inside your building. Make the proper adjustments to take a good picture. Then go inside and, without changing the speed setting, see what f-stop is required to take the same type picture there. If the setting is a lower number, you will know that the light inside is less than what you considered equal light conditions outside. This simple test helps prove how dark it really is inside a building.

Artificial light can help plants grow and should be used when light conditions inside are extremely bad. However, use the camera test when adding artificial light so that you can give the plants the amount they need.

The best answer to the light intensity problem is to use natural sunlight through windows. Plants will grow well when placed in sunny areas indoors. Use the camera test here, also. When taking the reading inside, however, do not point the camera at the window; instead, stand in front of the window and point it toward the area where you will place the plants.

Some precautions should be followed when plants are placed in direct sunshine:

- Use only plants that need bright light.
- Watch your watering schedule. When the sun's rays fall directly on the soil surface of the pot, the planting medium will dry through rapid surface evaporation as well as the normal transpiration from the leaves.
- Be careful when placing plants next to a window in the winter because heat radiation from the leaves to a cold sky may reduce the leaf-surface temperature to a dangerously low level.

There are other ways of improving a building's light to allow you to grow better plants. Overhead skylights brighten an area tremendously. Window greenhouses are helpful additions to any room, providing a fine environment for many plants that do poorly under normal house conditions. Many people are now constructing conservatories and greenhouses as a part of their buildings.

I built a free-standing greenhouse in my yard many years ago, and use it as a hospital for ailing plants which have suffered under my household conditions, as well as a growing house for blooming plants to bring inside our home on special occasions.

PLANT SELECTION

There is an almost limitless number of house plant types which are being propagated for growing indoors. Whether green plants, colorful leaf plants, or flowering plants, the choice is yours. You can be successful with them all, provided you try to grow them with the inhibiting factors I have mentioned in mind.

Choosing which house plants to buy is like landscaping your home or beginning a garden. You have two ways to approach the problem:

- You can choose plants which fit the cultural situation of a particular spot in your building. If the light is low, find a plant with a very low light requirement. If the room is cool, find a plant which grows well in low temperatures.
- Or you can choose a plant which completes the decorative look of the area and then adjust conditions to help it grow well. Perhaps a palm is ideal for a spot where you need height but there is too little light. One answer is to use enough artificial light to satisfy the needs of the plant.

Indoor plants can be attractive when carefully grown.

The important point to remember is that a dying or poorly growing plant will detract from rather than add to the beauty of a room. The plant list section of this chapter will guide you as you begin making your choices.

HEALTHY GROWING PRACTICES

I have stated that all plants which are grown indoors are natural in another place and another environment. All grow in the ground, with the exception of a few which have adapted themselves to growing in trees. None are ever native to a pot or planter, just as none are native to the inside of a building.

To be successful you must start with a good container and good soil, then plant correctly in the pot, water in the right way, fertilize with the correct nutrients, and finally control any insects and diseases which may attack your houseplants.

Choosing the Right Container

The container you choose must help your growing medium act like the soil in the plant's natural habitat.

- It must be large enough for the roots to grow well and to anchor sufficiently to hold up the top. It must provide enough soil to hold sufficient water, nutrients, and air for the plant's support.
- It must allow excess water to drain out of the bottom.
- It should be made of a material which is tough and resistant to cracking and breaking. It is best if it can "breathe" by being made of a porous material such as fired clay.

Choosing the Right Potting Soil

After selecting the correct pot for your plant you must decide which type of soil you will use as a growing medium for your plant. Observing the soil in our Malaysian jungle and calling upon many sad experiences at home in Sweet Apple, I have concluded that the only good media in which to grow houseplants are the so-called "soil-less" or "peat-light" soils. Choose a medium with the following characteristics:

- It should be light, and include a preponderance of peat moss, ground bark, vermiculite, and perlite.
- It should hold enough water for good growth but not enough to become soggy, a condition which encourages anaerobic or toxic gases to form.

Developing Good Watering Practices

Knowing when and how to water is of prime importance when growing house plants. If we look at the way nature waters its plants, we see that, except in a very few places in the world, rain comes on no strict schedule. Heavy rain may be followed by periods of no rain. Plants survive very well under nature's watering system. Here are some good rules to follow:

- Water when the plant and the soil in the pot need it, not on any arbitrary schedule.
- Water each time the surface of the soil in the pot feels dry to the touch.
- Water thoroughly each time you water, being sure that the entire root ball in the pot is damp.
- Water more often when plants are actively growing and when the humidity is low.
- Wilting of the plant is not necessarily an indication that the soil in the pot needs water. Too much water can cause root damage and low water uptake, both of which also result in wilting.

Developing a Good Fertilizing Program

Plants must have certain nutrients to grow well. In nature, billions of years of soil development have provided the vital nutrients for the plants which inhabit a particular area.

Plants taken away from their native habitat and placed inside our homes must also have nutrients. Since we provide a limited amount of soil in which the house plant must grow, we must constantly add these necessary nutrients to the soil in the pot.

Remember, when we apply nutrients for a plant's use, whether indoors or outdoors, we are not feeding the plant. Plants produce food to feed themselves. We are applying fertilizers to give the plant the nutrients it needs to produce its own food. The criteria for plant nutrients are:

- Use a soluble house plant fertilizer and apply as recommended in the watering solution.

- Use both organic and inorganic materials in your fertilizing program.
- Fertilize when the plant needs it, not on a strict year-round schedule. Plants need more fertilizer when growing rapidly and less when resting.
- Be careful not to over-fertilize. Both organic and inorganic fertilizer nutrients are made up of chemical salts which will burn the plant if applied too heavily or too often.

Controlling Insects and Diseases

Insects and diseases occur on house plants just as they do on garden plants. Though the dry air in our buildings reduces the incidence of disease, there may be attacks of insects like aphids, scale, mealybug, spider mites, thrips (mainly on flowering plants), larvae (soft worms) on the foliage, and sowbugs and pillbugs on the roots. Several excellent house plant insecticides are available for these problems. Take a sample of the affected portion of the plant or the plant itself to your local plantsman or county extension agent for identification and recommendation of control measures.

Handling the Transition Period

Twice a year, house plants go through their greatest trauma as you change from heating to air conditioning and vice versa. These sudden changes in humidity can cause severe problems. In the spring, or when the air conditioning is turned on, mist your plants several times a day or run the cold-air vaporizer during the daylight hours. Gradually reduce the number of mistings or number of hours in which the vaporizer runs until the roots have become active enough to replace the moisture being lost from the leaves.

In the fall, there is generally a lag time between when the air conditioner is turned off and the furnace is turned on. The trauma then is not as great, because the plants have time to adjust on their own. But you should watch them for signs of wilting of the succulent growth at the end of each branch. Apply the mist or run the vaporizer to help the plants adjust to their new situation.

GETTING STARTED

Now that you understand the basics, you need to apply that information as you begin your own adventure with house plants.

CHOOSING THE RIGHT PLANT

The first step is finding the plant which you like and which will fit into conditions where it will be placed. Most indoor plant stores and nurseries tag their plants with the conditions in which they do best. Before going to the plant shop, do the camera experiment described above and fix in your mind the *true* quality of light in the spot you have chosen for your plant.

If you should see an interesting or intriguing plant that you like, determine from the tag what conditions are required and decide if you have a suitable spot in which to place it.

The listings farther on in this chapter are a good guide and should help you start with some ideas before heading on your buying trip.

Most plants found in plant shops and nurseries have been expertly grown under ideal conditions. However, you should check each plant you are interested in for vigor, for presence of insects and diseases, and for damaged foliage which might indicate poor watering practices in the plant store or excessive handling. While you are at the nursery, ask the salesman to let you see the root ball; have him actually pull the plant out of the pot. If the roots are heavily matted against the outer edge of the ball of earth, it needs repotting and you should do it as soon as you get home. If the roots are barely visible or not heavily matted, the plant may continue growing as it is for some time.

SELECTING AN APPROPRIATE CONTAINER

Many times, the nursery container is not appropriate for your spot. If the plant needs repotting, now is the time to choose the right container following the suggestions above. If the plant does not need repotting you may wish to choose your new container, merely setting the pot and plant inside the new one without repotting.

There is a diversity in indoor plant materials which makes decorating fun.

Clay pots breathe and help plants grow better.

Plastic pots are easy to clean and attractive but do not breathe.

Hanging pots and baskets are excellent for they usually drain well.

Though repotting is not a difficult task, doing it correctly is most important. Purchase your soil mixture and fertilizer as well as the new container when you buy your new plant. Be sure you also have a glazed ceramic saucer in which to set your pot. This will prevent moisture from seeping through and ruining your furniture or floor.

There are many different kinds of pots available. An unglazed clay pot has very definite advantages. It is relatively inexpensive and has an earthy look which I find quite natural. The most important feature is that it "breathes." The fired clay is slightly porous; when it is dry, it allows much-needed air to enter the pot in minute amounts. This breathing helps the soil stay fresh in the pot and helps your plant grow better.

Since plastic pots do not breathe, more care is needed to prevent overwatering and stagnation of the soil. It is harder to water correctly in a

Ceramic pots should always have good drainage if you pot plants directly into them. They do not breathe.

A good way to handle a nondraining pot is to slip another draining pot inside.

A saucer is helpful to catch excess water, but fired clay saucers will allow some moisture to escape and should not be used directly on rugs or fine furniture.

Pots may be placed in waterproof planters.

plastic pot than in a clay pot, especially if your soil mixture is heavy. The advantages of a plastic pot are its low cost, ease in cleaning, lack of moisture seeping through, and difficulty in breaking.

Glazed ceramic pots are used a great deal since they are decorative and most attractive. But they will need the same kind of attention as a plastic pot and have the same disadvantages.

No matter what kind of pot you buy, be sure it will drain well. Good drain holes in the bottom of your growing container are essential. Planting in a pot without drainholes and then trying to prevent water stagnation in the bottom by using charcoal and gravel is not worth the effort and

Always use a light mixture which drains well such as this peat-light mixture.

expense. It seldom works satisfactorily. It is much better to slip a plant planted in a clay pot down inside a decorative pot so that you have the best of both worlds.

PURCHASING THE BEST POTTING SOIL

After choosing your new plant, you must decide whether to repot it before placing it in its growing spot. I have already mentioned the criteria for potting soils to be used with tropical house plants.

Remember always to use one of the "peat-light" potting mixtures. I have found they will prevent many difficulties house plants are apt to have. Because they are blends of very light materials, they hold sufficient moisture for growth, while at the same time they prevent excess water from remaining in the pot. This eliminates many root problems caused by the presence of anaerobic bacteria, which can be detected by the sour smell.

There are many "peat-light" mixtures on the market. I prefer those which include some added nutrients as well as a wetting agent, which helps the dry material to absorb moisture the first time water is added.

Stay away from heavy "jungle mixes." I have never seen a real jungle with soil that heavy!

TRANSPORTING THE PLANT

Though it may seem ridiculous, the trip home may be the most disastrous part of establishing a new plant.

Many of us like to buy lush tropical plants in the winter when so much of nature is dormant. Yet the cold temperatures can be very damaging. Try not to buy tropicals on a day when the weather is freezing. If you do, however, be sure the car is warm and take your plant straight home, avoiding stops where the car is left for long periods of time and the inside gets very cold.

Never take a lush green plant home with the top sticking out a window or hanging out of the trunk. The wind will dehydrate the leaves in a very short time and your plant can be seriously damaged.

I can attest to this. When we moved to Sweet Apple, I had a gorgeous six-foot-high Schefflera which Betsy and I had nurtured from a small

Don Hastings III getting ready to take his prize Ficus and its offspring back to Davidson College.

Load plants carefully in a car when transporting, even when taking home from a near-by nursery.

Do not let a large plant hang out of a window where the rushing air will dry the leaves. In the summer keep the car cool and in the winter keep it warm.

plant. It was so big that we had to put it on an open truck with our furniture. That was the end of our Schefflera! When we reached our new home, the leaves were brown, the stems shriveled, and no amount of pruning, watering, misting, and loving care could revive our wonderful plant.

EARLY PLANT CARE

Tropical plants are propagated and grown by nurserymen in greenhouses or in areas of the South where conditions are ideal all the time. They have prospered in places of high humidity and proper light. Experts have constantly monitored their need for moisture and fertilizer, and looked for the presence of insects and diseases, which are quickly controlled. These nurseries are the best possible substitutes for the plant's natural habitat.

Thus, the first few days your new baby is home in the environment where most of us live is traumatic for a tropical houseplant. Immediately after you arrive home, water the plant thoroughly before placing it where it will be growing.

When it is situated in its new spot, place a cold-air vaporizer nearby or begin a misting program to increase the humidity around the plant. Gradually reduce the time the vaporizer runs or the number of mistings to wean the plant away from this help. After about a week, your plant's roots will have started active growth and it can survive and grow on its own.

KEEPING HOUSEPLANTS GROWING

The joy of having living plants in a home cannot be measured. Now you can enjoy the freshness and beauty of nature all year. All that I have said so far is background for the marvelous opportunities found in learning to garden inside. Just like outdoor gardening, there are challenges, rewards, successes, and failures which make this part of gardening so worthwhile.

I have set forth the principles above. Now we must tend to the "nitty-gritty" which also can be fun and rewarding.

WATERING YOUR PLANTS

Unfortunately, improper watering is one of the main causes of failure with houseplants, and understanding how to water properly is of absolute importance in growing these plants successfully.

The secret is to develop a method of watering when the plant needs water and leaving it alone when it doesn't. I have a simple and almost

Leave surface of the soil below the lip of the pot so that you can fill with water and allow to slowly soak into the root ball.

Water plants in a sink where they may be thoroughly soaked and allowed to drain several times.

Fill the pot with water to the brim and allow it to soak in slowly. Do this several times.

After draining has finished, place the plant in its spot. Don't water again until the plant needs it.

On a warm day carry large plants outside where they may be properly watered without damaging rugs or floors.

foolproof method of watering house plants. Water a plant thoroughly by pouring slowly into the center of the root ball where the main stem emerges. Water several times until water comes freely through the drain hole. Do not water again until the surface of the soil in the pot is dry to the touch. Then water as before.

Betsy and I have developed an easy way to water pot plants. We take all the dry plants to the sink or the bath tub. Then we put each pot under a slowly running faucet and fill it to the rim with water. While it soaks in,

Fill the pot to the brim by slowly pouring water into the center of the pot.

Let the water soak into the root ball and come out through the drain hole.

we do the next pot. When all have been filled several times and water is coming out each drain hole, we leave all the pots on the drain board or in the tub overnight to prevent dripping on the rugs when they are taken back to their spots. This system works well and gives us excellent results with our house plants. The key, however, is the soil mixture, which allows excess water to flow through the pot. Using this method with heavy soil mixtures can be disastrous, so don't do it! If you are stuck with plants already potted in heavy soil, I recommend repotting if possible or using a moisture indicator stick and watering very carefully.

It is difficult, if not impossible, to try to put your plants on a strict watering schedule. Plants will need more water when it is colder outside than when it is milder because the furnace is running more and the air is drier. Plants need more water in the summer than in the winter because air conditioners dry the air more than furnaces do, and because summer days are longer, causing heavier growth which requires more water.

Nature does not water on a strict schedule either. Here in the South it rains and then we have periods without rain. These intervals may vary tremendously from a few days to several weeks. In the tropics it seldom rains every day, even during the rainy season. Plants over eons of time have developed methods for growing under these circumstances of wet and dry times and we, using pots in which to grow plants indoors, should be more like nature than like a computer program in our watering habits. We should let the soil in the pot dry out some before deluging with water once again. We have seen how varying conditions in the home and seasonal changes in the growth rate of the plant will affect the need for water. I boldly urge you to reject the advice seen in many places which flatly states that a given plant should be watered weekly or twice weekly or whatever. You will grow much better plants inside if you use your own judgment and follow the rules set forth above rather than somebody else's schedules.

This Pothos is happy with its growing conditions.

In all of *Gardening in the South,* I have stressed that we must understand the difference between wilting caused by apparently too little water, and wilting caused by the destruction of the root system by too much water. The same is just as true, perhaps more so, with plants in a pot. Overwatering is so serious a problem with houseplants that I can confidently state it is the leading cause of failure once a plant is established indoors. The best rule to remember is to underwater rather than take a chance of overwatering. Plants will recover quickly if the soil gets somewhat dry and they start to wilt. But they will have a hard time recovering at all if wilting is caused by a deterioration of the root system from overwatering.

In the above recommendations for types of pots and soil mixtures, I stressed using a light mixture which drains well, and a pot which has good drain holes, to prevent water from accumulating in the bottom of the pot, becoming stagnant, and allowing the development of harmful anaerobic bacteria in the potting mixture. A good soil mixture, a good pot, and a sensible program based on adding water when the plant needs it will go a very long way toward success with houseplants.

REPOTTING YOUR PLANTS

Indoor plants must be repotted at certain intervals whether they are repotted when purchased or not. Every few months when the plant is actively growing, lay it on its side. Lightly tap the sides of the pot with something firm, but be careful with a clay or ceramic pot which will crack easily. Slip the plant out of the pot by pulling the stem. Inspect the root system. If the roots are brown and matted it is time to repot; if they are white or not heavily matted you may wait awhile. While the ball is exposed I like to inspect it for soil insects and to smell it for indications of too much water (a sour smell). Sowbugs and pillbugs love to nest in the soil ball. If you see any, remove as much of the nest as possible and dust the pocket with Diazinon soil dust or some other good soil insecticide.

If you need to repot, get ready by choosing a new pot two sizes larger than the present one. Soak a clay pot for several hours in a tub of water to drive out as much air as possible. It is not necessary to soak a glazed ceramic pot. While the pot is soaking, get your soil ready. Peat-light soil mixtures are usually very dry and hard to wet the first time. I open the plastic bag and fill the bag with water. Let the soil absorb this water until it is thoroughly wet, even if you must rewater several times.

Place a piece of broken clay pot, concave side down, over the drain hole. Place several handfuls of the wet mixture in the bottom of the pot and set your plant in, ball and all, to see how much more soil you need so that the top of the ball will be at least an inch below the top of the lip of the pot. NEVER FILL THE POT WITH SOIL ALL THE WAY TO THE TOP OF THE LIP. The inch space at the top will prevent water from spilling over the lip when watering.

Hold the ball of the plant and with your fingers pull the matted roots until they are loose. If they are too tightly bound to do this easily, make a cut on each side of the ball with a sharp knife, pulling the roots loose as best you can. Reset the ball while packing the soil mixture underneath until the top is at the correct level. Now pour the loose soil mixture around the sides, packing with your fingers as you do. Hold the pot by the lip and tap downward on a piece of wood. This will settle the soil so that more may be added. When the soil is tightly packed around the ball and against the sides of the pot, water the plant thoroughly to settle the soil even more and remove any air pockets.

If you have read Volume I of *Gardening in the South,* you will recognize that this procedure is almost the same as for planting container-grown shrubs in the ground.

After repotting has been completed, I leave the plant in the best growing spot that I have for several weeks before returning it to the inside of my house. In the winter this is my greenhouse; in the summer it is on a special table under a tree outside. The roots are always damaged to some extent when repotting is done. Therefore, new root activity should take place before the plant goes back into the hostile environment of a building.

NURTURING YOUR PLANTS

I have stressed the importance of a good watering program because it is critical in keeping plants growing well. However, fertilizer and pest control programs are also most important to keep plants healthy and active. Sound familiar? It should, for this is what we have been learning to do correctly in our gardens outside. The only difference is that the indoor garden spot is a small pot and a building's environment is a poor substitute for what is found outside.

Even though most houseplants come from an environment where there is relatively little difference in temperature throughout the year, there will be a difference in their growth rate as our seasons change in the southern United States. Growth differences from spring until fall and winter are very noticeable in many common house plant types. You must adjust your fertilizing schedules to fit the natural growth of the plant. It might be quite sufficient to fertilize every three or four weeks in the fall and winter when growth is sparse, but quite insufficient in the spring and early summer when growth is heavy.

Fertilize regularly when your plants are beginning to grow actively and continue until they slow their growth. Then fertilize sparsely until active growth begins again. I use nothing but soluble fertilizers for my main fertilizing program, but I intersperse it with applications of organic fertilizers such as fish oil emulsion, garden tea (the liquid formed when a half-filled bucket of dehydrated cattle manure is filled with water and allowed to settle), plus a good organic promoting material such as OST. The soluble fertilizers give the plant the nutrients required for growth; the organics keep the soil conditioned properly for root development.

As stated before, insects are the major problems which the indoor gardener faces. Many of these can seriously damage a plant. Mealybugs, spider mites, scale, leafhoppers, aphids, and thrips on flowers, slugs, and soil insects such as sowbugs and pillbugs may be a problem. Watch your plants carefully and start a control program before the problem overwhelms the plant. Once a plant is thoroughly infested, it may be better to discard it than to risk spreading the pest to other nearby plants. Your nurseryman or plant shop operator is the best source of information about up-to-date controls of these pests. Many house plants by their nature are sensitive to some chemicals commonly used outside on garden plants. Avoid these unless they are recommended specifically for house plants. Many chemicals for the garden outside have rather unpleasant smells and should only be used, even if recommended, when the plants are taken outside for spraying.

As with all chemicals, use sparingly and only when needed. Use only as recommended on the container and always wear gloves and a face mask when spraying, especially in a confined area.

Insects are a major threat to beautiful houseplants.

Insect damage will make your plants unsightly.

ALL ABOUT HOUSEPLANTS
FOR THE SOUTH

When preparing much of this chapter, I faced out the office window in my house in Kuala Lumpur, Malaysia. Immediately outside was my constant companion, a beautiful palm tree. Why, I thought, shouldn't it be on my plant list? But why stop there? What about every plant in the yard and Betsy's Orchids? What about Datin Loy's plants and those outside my company office window? I wanted every one in this book because by then they were familiar to me, and I was sure they were just as good for Sweet Apple as the ones found in nurseries and plant shops nearby.

If I did include them all, however, the plant list would be virtually useless to you, for how could you ever find these constant companions of mine? The Sealing Wax Palm, the most spectacular of all palms, is one I have never seen in our plant shops. Expediency requires that I show a few in pictures here, but refrain from listing them as possibilities until someday they are discovered by our propagators and nurserymen.

The lists which follow are necessarily limited in scope, but so many plants are being grown, you should be able to find them in our local nurseries and plant shops.

I have not dwelt on flowering plants, either, since few of them perform for any length of time. I am sure that the lovers of African Violets will be upset when I mention them only as a possibility for the average homeowner. In a volume such as this, there is not space enough to go into detail about such fine groups of plants as African Violets, Impatiens, Orchids and Bromiliads used as houseplants when I know that only a few of you will ever grow any of them and fewer yet will grow them all. For those who cherish these lovely plants, let me say that, grown well, they can certainly be a delight to the indoor gardener. Having mentioned them in passing, I hope that you will be excited enough about these generalities to pursue these plants on your own.

It is difficult to present houseplants in an orderly manner. In the first place, tropical plant names are more confused and disorderly than other plant types. Each country has its own common names for its more widely-grown plants, and our plant introducers have often created "saleable" names when they have placed a new plant in commerce. Because plant importers have often misidentified the plants being brought into commerce, they arrive in plant shops with wholly inappropriate "scientific" names.

To be as accurate as possible under the circumstances, I have relied heavily on my old authority *Hortus Third*, as well as the good advice of Bernardino Ballesteros and Dr. Oscar Opina. Let us hope that you and I are on the same wavelength and you can decipher from the following lists what you wish to know about the houseplants which you will see in plant shops and nurseries.

In order to make it easy to find the right plant, I have subdivided the list into the following groups:
- Plants grown mainly for their attractive foliage
- Succulents
- Flowering plants
- Inside-outside plants

Plants we grow inside are basic landscaping material in the tropics.

Betsy Hastings with one of her orchids in Kuala Lumpur

The unusual Heliconia is an excellent inside-outside plant.

Aglaonema is a useful houseplant.

Pothos is grown inside for its foliage.

The Hibiscus makes an excellent inside-outside plant.

Streptocarpus is a good inside flowering plant.

A spectacular Sealing Wax Palm at St. Francis Xavier Church in Kuala Lumpur.

AGLAONEMA or SILVER EVERGREEN, GOLDEN EVERGREEN
Aglaonema commutatum

Use: Large foliage plant
Height: 3 feet or more
Shape: Bushy clumps
Origin: Southeast Asia
Light Requirements: Moderate and diffused
Humidity Requirements: High
Temperature Requirements: Warm
Unique Characteristics: The striking variegated leaves and bushy habit make it ideal as a large pot plant.

I learned to like the Aglaonemas while in Malaysia where they are frequently seen as a common pot plant for both inside and outside. They are easy to grow if they are given plenty of humidity to prevent edge "burn" or browning and not too much sun. They need well-drained soil and frequent fertilizer when in active growth.

There are many different foliage variants of silver and green, gold and green, and various silver spots and streaks. Though I have never seen many of these variants here at home, I hope that some of the cultivars like "White Rajah" will find their way into our plant shops.

The Aglaonemas produce large clumps in the pot and end up after several years of growth as large, bushy, three-foot-high clumps where the leaves hide the stalks, making it much more attractive than the Chinese Evergreen, Aglaonema modestum, which is commonly grown here.

ALUMINUM PLANT
Pilea cadierei

Use: Foliage plant
Height: 10 to 12 inches
Shape: Compact
Origin: Vietnam
Light Requirements: Low to medium
Humidity Requirements: High
Temperature Requirements: Warm
Unique Characteristics: Unusual foliage

The Aluminum Plant is an interesting variegated plant with a compact habit and bushy growth. It will survive in moderately low light and should not be placed in a cold window. It may be propagated from tip cuttings. There is a miniature form which does well in terrariums.

❦ ARTILLERY PLANT
Pilea microphylla

Use: Foliage plant
Height: 8 to 12 inches
Shape: Low and bushy
Origin: Tropical America
Light Requirements: Medium
Humidity Requirements: High
Temperature Requirements: Warm
Unique Characteristics: Dainty foliage covering stems. Its appearance is somewhat like that of a succulent though its culture is not.

The Artillery Plant is relatively easy to grow if it has plenty of humidity and a well-drained soil which will not get soggy as a result of the frequent waterings which it needs. It may be grown in terrariums. The best results come from placing the pot on wet pebbles to increase the humidity. The Artillery Plant is attractively used as a border plant in indoor planters or in pots around an indoor plant grouping.

❦ ASPIDISTRA or CAST-IRON PLANT
Aspidistra elatior

Use: Foliage plant in tough situations
Height: 2 feet or more
Shape: Thick, upright
Origin: Japan
Light Requirements: Minimum
Humidity Requirements: Low to moderate
Temperature Requirements: Withstands moderately low temperatures in the winter
Unique Characteristics: Very tough, easy to grow

Many of you may have seen this tough plant growing outdoors in the deep South, especially along the Gulf Coast and in Florida. There are many outside mass plantings in Mobile under heavily-foliaged trees.

Its name, Cast-Iron Plant, is appropriate because it grows easily and has a wide tolerance to poor household conditions. It will last for many years if kept moderately damp when actively growing in the summer and somewhat drier when resting in the winter. Fertilize frequently in the summer when it is actively growing.

Aspidistra may be easily divided in the spring to provide new plantings.

❦ BABY'S TEARS
Soleirolia Soleirolii

Use: Small, bushy foliage plant
Height: 3 to 5 inches

Shape: Low, trailing
Origin: The Mediterranean area
Light Requirements: Medium
Humidity Requirements: High
Temperature Requirements: Medium
Unique Characteristics: It is a very dainty, easy-to-grow trailing plant.

Baby's Tears is popular as a potted or hanging plant which will do well in most inside conditions where additional humidity can be provided. A friend had one hanging over the kitchen sink where the humidity was high and the light through the kitchen window helped it to grow profusely.

Baby's Tears has a tendency to grow a bit unsightly in the winter when the humidity is low, but it is quickly restored in the spring with some careful pruning to remove dead wood and leaves and a good fertilizing as new growth starts.

❦ BANANA, DWARF CAVENDISH
Musa acuminata cv. 'Dwarf Cavendish'

Use: Tall, upright floor plant
Height: Up to 10 feet
Shape: Tree
Origin: Asia
Light Requirements: High
Humidity Requirements: High
Temperature Requirements: Warm, minimum of 65 degrees
Unique Characteristics: Huge attractive leaves; sometimes the plant forms unique flowers and on rare occasions fruits will appear.

The only Banana really suited to inside a building is the Dwarf Cavendish. It grows tolerably well but must be in just the right spot or it is not attractive at all.

Grow Bananas in large (really huge) pots in extremely well-drained soil. Add one part sand or perlite to three parts of the regular peat-lite mixture.

Place the pot in as much light as possible but avoid direct western sun through a window. A conservatory or in a place brightened with a sky-light window is best. Keep the humidity and temperature high. Fertilize regularly with a balanced, high potency soluble house plant fertilizer. Keep the soil moist at all times but do not ever let it become soggy.

Occasionally a flower cluster will form and, rarely, Bananas will follow. Once the stalk has flowered and fruited, it is sterile and will produce no more. Take a side sprout off the main plant and root it for your new Banana production, leaving the old plant as something green in the house until it becomes ratty.

Bananas are subject to most of the common house plant insects, especially aphids and mites. Keep the plant sprayed regularly when these attack.

For further information about Bananas, see "Inside-Outside Plants" at the end of these plant lists.

BEGONIA
Begonia sp.

Use: Foliage and flowering plant
Height: Various, depending on the type
Shape: Various, depending on the type
Origin: Widespread in tropical and subtropical areas
Light Requirements: Moderate to diffused
Humidity Requirements: High
Temperature Requirements: Moderate to high
Unique Characteristics: Attractive foliage and blossoms

BEGONIA VARIETIES

There are so many wonderful begonias being grown today that it is difficult to choose an approach to this group of plants when discussing their use as houseplants. Generally speaking, many of our common garden begonias may do quite well inside the house when properly handled. I have grown garden begonias inside simply to overwinter my favorite colors, and find that they survive nicely and add a lot to our home during the dreary winter.

We can divide the more common types into groups as follows:

1. **Fibrous-rooted begonias**, which include:
   - The *wax* group, which is the common garden begonia
   - The *cane-forming* types, including the angel-wing begonias
   - The *hairy-leaf* begonias
2. **Rhizomatous-rooted begonias**, which include the Rex Begonias grown mainly for their bright foliage
3. **Tuberous-rooted begonias**, which encompass a large number of spectacular flowering types including the double Camellia-flowering begonias

From this list we can assemble an excellent group of foliage and flowering begonias for inside use. Of the above types, the easiest to grow inside are the fibrous-rooted, cane-types, and the rhizomatous-rooted types, including the more common and spectacular *Begonia rex-cultorum* or Rex Begonia.

One should begin the culture of the tuberous-rooted begonias with some caution as they are rather sensitive and are susceptible to a number of insect and growth problems.

Another way to approach the growing of begonias inside is to find types whose culture fulfills a definite function or cross-function in our total gardening scheme. Three functions would be:

- **Double-use culture**: those grown as garden plants in summer and houseplants in the winter
- **Inside-outside plants**: those grown as pot plants inside in the winter and on porches, terraces, or outside living areas in the summer
- **Inside plants**: those grown inside all the time

As mentioned above, I have made it a practice over many years to lift and pot some of my prize wax-leaf garden begonias as well as to make a number of cuttings from plants which I wish to have again the next year. Keeping the larger

The hairy-leaf begonias make excellent indoor plants.

A tall, cane-type, angel-wing begonia makes an excellent houseplant.

Garden begonias may be cut back, potted, and used as indoor flowering plants.

This begonia has a serrated leaf.

The garden coleus grow well inside.

Make cuttings from your garden coleus early in the fall to have colorful plants in the winter.

plants alive and growing adds a great deal of color to our house and gives me the opportunity of making more cuttings prior to the new growing season. I have also found that rooting a few cuttings in the early fall, prior to the first cold weather, gives me a number of fresh, healthy plants for the house. These do even better than the lifted mother plants. By spring these young plants have grown enough to provide cuttings for as many new plants as I will need in my flower bed.

The cane-type or angel-wing begonias make excellent year-round potted plants which Betsy and I use on the porch during the summer and in the living room during the winter. I particularly like the *B. corallina* group which has a number of long 6- to 8-foot canes and dark green-spotted leaves with a bright red reverse. We have had one in a huge pot for years and have had very little difficulty in keeping this tall plant as one of the finest specimens in our whole houseplant collection. These plants will survive inside during the entire year once they are adapted to a certain spot and are growing well.

The *B. rex-cultorum* or Rex Begonias are often grown strictly as houseplants. Their attractive and colorful leaves are a cheerful addition to indoor plant groups.

Begonias, of whatever type, should be grown inside carefully with an eye on the humidity and water. None like to be dry, but too much watering will certainly damage the roots. Use a peat-light potting mixture and soak thoroughly each time you water. Water when the surface of the soil in the pot is beginning to feel dry to the touch. A humidifier is very useful when placed near begonias for they do not perform well in a dry atmosphere. Fertilize on a regular basis when the plants are actively growing, and reduce fertilizer to a subsistence level (half application, half as frequently) during the dark days of winter when growth is minimal.

❦ CHINESE EVERGREEN
Aglaonema modestum

Use: Foliage plant
Height: 2 to 3 feet
Shape: Upright
Origin: China, Thailand
Light Requirements: High
Humidity Requirements: Normal to high
Temperature Requirements: Warm
Unique Characteristics: Easily grown green plant with little effort needed to keep it healthy

The Chinese Evergreen is one of those foolproof plants that are as good a first houseplant venture as any except perhaps Aspidistra or Mother-in-law's Tongue. There are many types of plants which are more attractive and will serve a situation better, but few can be grown as easily.

I much prefer the Aglaonema commutatum mentioned above, which is much less leggy in appearance and, to me, a far superior plant to this one.

🌱 CITRUS—ORANGE, LEMON, KUMQUAT, CALAMONDIN AND THE LIKE
Citrus sp.

Use: Decorative foliage plant
Height: Various
Shape: Upright from bushy to tree form
Origin: Various
Light Requirements: High
Humidity Requirements: High
Temperature Requirements: Moderate to warm
Unique Characteristics: Many will bear fruit when carefully grown

A foliage plant is a great addition to a house; a foliage and flowering plant is even better. A foliage and flowering plant which bears fruit is perhaps the ultimate. The citrus group plants come as close to being complete plants as we find for indoor gardening. They have attractive foliage, pleasantly scented flowers, and if carefully grown they will have brightly colored fruit.

Many of us started citrus from seed when we were children, and this is still an ideal way to have a pleasant gardening experience inside. A mature grapefruit will yield many seeds which may be dried and planted in a pot. Oranges, kumquats, calamondins, and lemons all sprout easily from a seed removed from the fruit. You can buy fairly large citrus plants in nurseries and plant shops. Near Christmas, the bushy calamondins and kumquats, with their bright colors, are also available.

No matter how you obtain your citrus, growing it will take some effort. Citrus plants need high humidity and good light conditions. Careful attention must be paid to growing them well with a fertilizing schedule which follows their times of active growth. They must be planted in well-drained soil which is never allowed to dry out. If it does, the leaves will quickly drop and the succulent stem tips will dry up. When in flower, they must be misted to keep up the humidity, or the flowers will fall off before pollinating. Pollination should be completed by hand using a fine artist's brush to be sure that the pollen falls to the stigma. As the fruit develops, the plant will need more fertilizer and water since the ripening fruit is putting much stress on the plant.

Spider mites may become a problem so be on the watch for a change in the color and appearance of the leaves. If they are present, take your plant outside on a warm day and spray with a good miticide recommended by your garden dealer. If this is impossible, spray with a recommended houseplant insect spray.

CITRUS VARIETIES

TALL TREE FORM	SMALL TREE FORM TO BUSH FORM	SMALL BUSH FORM
Grapefruit	Meyer Lemon*	Kumquat*
Orange	Calamondin	
Satsuma*		

*Easy to grow

🌱 COFFEE PLANT
Coffea arabica

Use: Bush to small tree foliage plant
Height: 4 feet or more
Shape: Bush to tree
Origin: Tropical Africa
Light Requirements: Medium
Humidity Requirements: Medium/High, use a mist or vaporizer
Temperature Requirements: Moderate to warm
Unique Characteristics: Attractive foliage and a possibility of producing the red coffee beans

The Coffee Plant is another interesting addition to the indoor gardening experience. The idea of growing something as common as coffee beans inside the home gives this plant an appeal that it otherwise does not deserve for there are certainly more beautiful houseplants to grow. However, it is excellent as a challenge and will certainly add interest to your plantings inside.

🌱 COLEUS
Coleus Blumei and *Coleus X hybridus*

Use: Brightly colored foliage plant
Height: 6 inches to over 2 feet
Shape: Bushy
Origin: Mainly Java and the Philippines, though hybrids have originated in cultivation
Light Requirements: High
Humidity Requirements: Moderate to high
Temperature Requirements: Medium
Unique Characteristics: Noted for the various leaf forms and the bright coloration

The Coleus need no introduction to the average gardener who uses them extensively in outside plantings. Because of their tolerance to shade, they are adapted to the inside of the house, provided they are placed where they receive higher humidity than is normally found.

Coleus may be treated in a similar manner to the Begonias; grow the plants in the garden during the summer and lift them into pots for culture in the house during the winter. You may also take cuttings to start fresh new plants for overwintering.

🌱 CORN PLANT
Dracaena fragrans 'Massangeana'

(See *Dracaena*)

CREEPING FIG
Ficus pumila

Use: Trailing or climbing foliage plant
Height: 2 to 3 inches maximum
Shape: Flat
Origin: East Asia
Light Requirements: Moderate
Humidity Requirements: Medium
Temperature Requirements: Medium to warm
Unique Characteristics: Flat creeping habit and attractive foliage

The Creeping Fig or Fig Vine is well known in the South, having been grown outside in Florida and the Gulf Coast for many years. In Atlanta, there have been many plantings in protected areas which have survived most of our colder winters only to be killed when the arctic blasts drop the temperature below zero. Sometimes, however, the roots will start new shoots which will quickly replace the destroyed vines.

You can grow a Fig as a houseplant for years with no difficulty, provided you give it a higher than normal humidity and a spot with moderate light. In the right place it can be used as a clinging vine to cover unsightly walls.

The dainty leaves, flat growth habit, and clinging ability make it an interesting houseplant for pots or hanging baskets.

Some of the most beautiful plantings I have ever seen are in Singapore, where it is used as a cover for the stark and ugly concrete bridge supports on the freeways.

DRACAENAS
Dracaena sp.

There are many Draecenas with various leaf forms that are used as houseplants. In fact these are some of our most popular indoor plants.

There is very little problem in growing Dracaenas provided you start with a good potting mixture and a pot large enough to hold up the rapidly-growing plant which can easily become top-heavy. It will tolerate rather dry humidity provided you mist the plant regularly. Water thoroughly and then water again when the surface of the soil in the pot begins to feel dry to the touch.

Overwatering can cause root deterioration very quickly and the edges of the leaves will begin to turn brown exactly like when the plant dries out. If edge browning occurs, first check for overwatering if you have not knowingly let the plant dry out. Turn the pot on its side and slip the ball of soil out. Check for soggy, sour-smelling soil. If this is the case, remove the soil from the roots and repot in a mixture which drains better. If the soil seems all right but instead of wet it is dry despite your watering program, check the roots for evidence that the plant is pot-bound. Repot in a larger container.

The green Corn Plant is easy to grow inside.

The Creeping Fig will grow well inside.

Dracaena, or Corn Plant, grows very large. This one shows why they must be grown in a large pot indoors.

Dracaena in Kuala Lumpur

A huge multi-stem Corn Plant in Singapore at ultimate height

The common Dracaena marginata

Cultivars of D. marginata found in Southeast Asia

Dracaena surculosa, called Japanese Bamboo in the Orient, takes very low light.

Dieffenbachia in Kuala Lumpur

Dieffenbachia in Green Park, Makati, Philippines

CORN PLANT
Dracaena fragrans 'Massangeana' and other cultivars

Use: Tall foliage plant
Height: Up to 6 feet
Shape: Tall, tree-like
Origin: Upper Guinea
Light Requirements: Low to medium
Humidity Requirements: Medium
Temperature Requirements: Warm
Unique Characteristics: The tall canes topped with long corn-like leaves make an interesting accent planting.

Follow the general instructions for care of Dracaenas, but be aware of these additional tips on care.

The lower leaves of all Corn Plants will eventually lose their function and die. This is no cause for alarm; it is a rather natural thing. These leaves should be removed when they become unsightly. When the plant becomes too tall and leggy for your taste, cut it back to the height you like, even if you remove all the leaves. You will soon get new sprouts coming from a side bud and a new top will result.

Fertilize Corn Plants by following their growth rate, using more when in active growth and less in the winter when growth is slow.

Keep the foliage of the Corn Plant clean by washing with a soapy solution, followed by a thorough rinsing with clear water to remove all the soap residue. This will help keep insects, especially mites and mealybugs, under control.

OTHER DRACAENAS

Dracaena marginata
D. cincta or *D. concinna*

This beautiful narrow-leaf Dracaena has red-margined leaves.

Dracaena Godseffiana
D. surculosa

The Gold-dust Dracaena has attractive white-spotted and marbled leaves.

DUMB CANE
Dieffenbachia maculata and many cultivars

Use: Tall foliage plant
Height: 4 feet or more
Shape: Tall, tree shape
Origin: Central and South America
Light Requirements: Moderate
Humidity Requirements: Medium
Temperature Requirements: Warm

Unique Characteristics: An attractive cane plant with the unusual attribute of exuding a substance from the canes and leaves which can cause paralysis of the throat if ingested, hence, the name "Dumb Cane." The juice of the leaves may also cause skin irritation. It is best kept away from small children, especially toddlers who like to chew on everything in sight.

The Dieffenbachias are extremely attractive upright plants which will eventually grow large enough to attain a stalky, tree-like appearance. They are used much the same as the Dracaenas listed before and the Cordylines listed later under "Ti" plants.

Their culture is similar to the Dracaenas. Overwatering is the greatest cause of problems, though dirty, dusty leaves invite insects and diseases. Wiping clean with a mild soapy solution followed by a thorough washing with clear water will help control insects and keep your plant looking good.

FALSE ARALIA
Dizygotheca elegantissima

Use: Tall foliage plant
Height: 4 feet or more
Shape: Tall, tree shape
Origin: New Caledonia
Light Requirements: Moderate
Humidity Requirements: Medium to high
Temperature Requirements: Warm
Unique Characteristics: The feathery foliage

The False Aralia is one of the more popular accent plants for the home. It grows large and eventually the trunk and lower branches may become substantial, giving a truly unique structure. Its main attraction is the feathery foliage, which is bronze when young.

The False Aralia is not difficult to grow if planted in a medium which drains well but retains sufficient moisture. Overwatering, however, can be disastrous. Spider mites may also be a problem and should be watched for and treated before the infestation gets out of control.

FATSHEDERA
X Fatshedera Lizei

Use: Upright, semi-climbing tub plant for foliage
Height: 6 feet
Shape: Upright
Origin: Originated in cultivation (France)
Light Requirements: Medium
Humidity Requirements: Medium to high
Temperature Requirements: Cool to warm

Unique Characteristics: Heavy, large ivy-like leaves and upright habit. A tough plant. Cv. 'Variegata' is a white-margined leaf form which must not be put in too much light.

Fatshedera is a cross between Japanese Aralia and English Ivy and is used upon occasion in the lower South as an outside garden plant. It will survive quite nicely inside if it is grown in a rather large tub and in a spot where other similar plants are grown under high humidity.

It is rather coarse and not as attractive as the smaller-leaf English Ivies but it is easier to train into a tall tub plant. It is rather good as an inside-outside plant for areas of the South where the temperature drops below twenty degrees during the winter. Otherwise it may be safely left outside.

🌿 FATSIA or JAPANESE ARALIA
Fatsia japonica

Use: Large, exotic foliage plant
Height: 4 feet or more
Shape: Upright
Origin: Japan
Light Requirements: Moderate
Humidity Requirements: Average to high
Temperature Requirements: Cool to very warm
Unique Characteristics: Exotic, tropical-looking plant with a bold appearance

The Fatsia is a bold, interesting plant best grown in a large tub and used to give an exotic look to a grouping of tropical plants in a room or as a single accent plant.

It is widely grown outside in upper Florida and the coastal lower South and may be grown, also, as an attractive inside-outside plant.

Use a high peat mixture or add an additional amount of peat moss to your regular peat-light mixture. It grows best in moist (but not soggy) soil.

TRUE FERNS

There is no more beautiful group of indoor plants than the ferns and fern-like plants that can be grown inside the house. The woodsy, natural feeling these plants give is unique.

One must remember, however, that these are plants of the forest and as such they require a much higher humidity than many other houseplants we grow. In the old days, people had ferneries where these plants would grow and be displayed in a more natural setting and culturally satisfactory environment. For most of us, this is not possible, and so we must alter our environment to keep these wonderful plants growing at their best.

The basic needs of these plants might seem simple yet the environment in which we live is not an environment which they like. It is, therefore, necessary to provide special care and to cater to their specific needs.

Huge tree ferns grow wild in Malaysia.

True ferns native to Southern forests may be potted for indoors.

Ferns grow well as inside-outside plants.

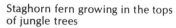
Staghorn fern growing in the tops of jungle trees

A tree fern in Green Park, Makati, Manila

HUMIDITY

Ferns are plants of the forests and stream banks and must have high humidity to survive. An area of the home which can be devoted to these plants is best. In that area a pebble layer would be laid on a watertight surface and kept damp all the time. Do not cover the rocks or allow the pots to be sitting in water. If this is not possible, the plants should be set in groups or with other high humidity plants among which a cold-air vaporizer is placed.

SOIL

Ferns grow best in fibrous, well-drained soil which holds moisture but can never become soggy, a condition which is deadly. A peat-light soil which has an abundance of sphagnum peat moss, ground bark, perlite and vermiculite is ideal. The goal is to keep the soil lightly moist at all times. A fern pot usually has extra drain holes to allow the water not held by the soil to drain out.

WATERING

Ferns should have an ample supply of water at all times but the pot *must* drain well and release the excess water. Water them thoroughly and be sure to allow the pots to drain after you are finished. I like to water my ferns in the sink and leave them sitting over the drain for several hours before putting them back in their place. The surface of the soil in the pot should still feel damp to the touch when you water again.

FERTILIZING

The roots of ferns are not as extensive as those of most other houseplants, and they are quite sensitive to excess fertilizer. Use a special fern fertilizer or regular houseplant fertilizer at one-half strength. Fish oil emulsion is ideal to alternate with your regular houseplant fertilizer.

LIGHT

These are plants of the forest and as such grow best in low light. This does not mean in a dark spot in the room, however. They do need some light and do well in a room with eastern or northern exposure where they can be closer to a window.

DRAFTS

Keep ferns away from heat vents, fans, air conditioners or windows and doors which might create a draft. Heavy air movement damages them.

PESTS

Ferns may be attacked by several insects, especially scale, mites and mealybugs. A careful watch should be kept for these pests since the fronds of ferns may be sensitive to many chemicals and control is difficult.

Scale can be severe and I have found the only practical way to control it is to cut out all infested fronds and treat the remaining with insecticidal soap. Then I apply a systemic insecticide to the soil.

Mealybug is best controlled when it first starts. Soak a cotton swab in alcohol and touch each of the culprits. That will kill them. Heavy infestations should be treated like scale.

Spider mites may become a problem, especially if other plants become infested. Wash the plants thoroughly with an insecticidal soap. If this fails to give control, then ask your nurseryman for a Kelthane formulation which is safe for ferns.

DISEASES

There is seldom any disease problem with ferns. However, many people confuse the brown spore formations on the backs of the leaves as either a disease or perhaps even scale. These formations are the natural manner of reproduction for the fern and should be cherished and not treated.

A tremendous number of ferns are suitable as indoor pot plants or inside-outside plants. Your local botanical garden or fern society will help you get started with these exciting and wonderful plants. I list a few which I have grown successfully, but this list is in no way exhaustive and should be taken only as a beginning point.

BIRD'S NEST FERN
Asplenium nidus

Use: Large pot plant
Height: 4 feet or more
Shape: Vase
Origin: Tropical Asia
Light Requirements: Moderate
Humidity Requirements: Medium to high
Temperature Requirements: Warm
Unique Characteristics: This huge fern is spectacular and worth every effort
   to grow

The Bird's Nest Fern is so spectacular when grown well that one might say it is incomparable. It is really unlike almost any other plant, yet it is a fern just like you see in the woods. My first sight of them was in high trees in Malaysia growing abundantly. Some of the larger trees would have eight or ten colonies.

We rescued several of these from fallen trees and potted them for our office. At home in Kuala Lumpur we had a beautiful specimen growing right beside the entrance to the house. It does grow big and should be used only where it can grow to its full size.

The Bird's Nest Fern grows in a mass of sphagnum-like material high in a tree where the only water it receives is from the rain. This gives a clue as to how they are best grown. The soil in the pot should be light and loose, preferably one of the peat-light mixtures. The soil should drain extremely well, and the plant should never be overwatered to the point of being soggy.

However, the humidity in the top of a tree in the jungle is very high due to the huge amount of transpiration from the leaves. Therefore, a Bird's Nest Fern will grow best when given extra humidity with frequent mistings or placed near a cold-air vaporizer.

A Bird's Nest fern grows in the top of a jungle tree in Malaysia.

John Huyck and the author rescued this Bird's Nest fern from a feld tree. It shows the mass of sphagnum-like material in which it was growing.

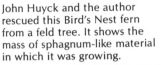

With good humidity a Bird's Nest fern grows well inside.

The Bird's Nest fern will grow in its own sphagnum-like root mass, as well as in a pot.

157

In the top of a dense tree it is not very bright and a Bird's Nest Fern should never be in direct sun or the leaves will soon burn at the tips and edges. They also lose their rich green color in too bright a spot.

Inside the house, they benefit from being in a cluster of plants where the humidity is easier to keep high. Growing on a pebble base which can be kept damp is of great help along with a vaporizer placed unobtrusively in the grouping.

Like all ferns, the demand for water and fertilizer in the pot is greater in the spring, summer and fall than in the resting period of winter. However, never let the plant dry out, and I like to maintain the fertility in the pot during this resting time by using fish oil emulsion.

BOSTON FERN
Nephrolepis exaltata cv. 'Bostoniensis'

Use: Table or stand plant or in hanging baskets
Height: 3 feet in height and length
Shape: Bushy to semi-trailing
Origin: Widespread in the tropics
Light Requirements: Medium
Humidity Requirements: High
Temperature Requirements: Warm
Unique Characteristics: The long arching fronds and heavy growth

I just wish that I could be as successful with this lovely fern as some of the country ladies who grew outstanding specimens in their homes which I used to visit as a youngster. Perhaps it was their innate green thumbs or the lack of central heat or air conditioning. Whatever it was, I shall always remember these huge plants sitting on fern stands in their homes. On a dreary winter day, they were a lovely sight.

Mine grow well enough on the porch during the summer, but the winter inside does them in. Mine always look ratty and are relegated to a shady spot in the greenhouse where they sit until spring when Betsy or I remove all the bad leaves and start them over. I think my fern spot is just too dry for the Boston Fern.

Start with a single, well grown, small one in a clay fern pot using the soil mixture described above. Leave it alone while it fills the pot and do not repot until absolutely necessary.

CLIMBING FERN
Lygodium palmatum

Use: Table plant with support or climber
Height: Many feet when growing well
Shape: Climbing
Origin: Eastern United States
Light Requirements: Medium
Humidity Requirements: Medium
Temperature Requirements: Cool in winter, warm in the summer
Unique Characteristics: The climbing habit and lacy foliage

This plant is described in the section on vines for it is widely grown outside, especially in the lower South where it is an evergreen.

I have also grown this as a houseplant and find it quite satisfactory and most interesting, for when it is happy, it will climb up anything it can find. It does well when grown on a bark slab or fern root post. Its first tendrils must be attached to something (it is a twining vine) but soon it will find a way to twine and creep up the support.

MAIDENHAIR FERN
Adiantum Raddianum, many cultivars

Use: Table plant
Height: 8 to 12 inches
Shape: Rounded to bushy
Origin: Brazil
Light Requirements: Low to medium
Humidity Requirements: High
Temperature Requirements: Warm
Unique Characteristics: Very unusual in form and shape but difficult to grow

Good luck with this plant! The Maidenhair Fern is perhaps the most beautiful of all, but it is as temperamental as any plant we grow inside. I say this while knowing many indoor gardeners who have great success with what seems to be the greatest of ease. I think the secret is to grow it like all ferns but be lucky enough to have a spot which it likes. I just don't seem to have such a spot, and most who have tried don't either. If you are successful, you have achieved a remarkable green thumb with just one plant.

SQUIRREL'S FOOT FERN, RABBIT'S FOOT FERN
Davallia sp.

Use: Table plant
Height: 12 to 18 inches
Shape: Rounded to spreading, often ball shaped
Origin: Various
Light Requirements: Medium
Humidity Requirements: Moderate
Temperature Requirements: Warm
Unique Characteristics: The unusual feet which cling to the sides of the pot or ball

Several of these ferns produce fuzzy "feet" which give the attractive plant a most unusual appearance. The one which I had for years had so many "feet" hanging onto the lip and sides of the pot that hardly any of the clay could be seen. It was one of our favorite plants.

These are not hard to grow; in fact, they are easier for me than the Boston Fern. The main problem is scale which will ruin a plant very quickly if left uncontrolled. I found excellent control with the use of a systemic insecticide in the soil.

The Maidenhair fern is beautiful but somewhat difficult to grow inside.

The "feet" of a Squirrel's-foot fern

Sprengeri Fern as an inside planting

A Sprengeri fern at Los Banos, Philippines

The common Southern fig as a houseplant

Swedish Ivy

Many other true ferns are seen from time to time in plant shops. Their absence from this list in no way indicates their worth. Tree ferns, table ferns, other climbing ferns, other "feet" ferns are all worthwhile. They should be grown with the same general principles as stated above. Try many and you will find a few which are to your liking and will do well in your home.

Fern-Like Plants

ASPARAGUS FERN or ASPARAGUS PLUMOSA
Asparagus setaceus, many cultivars

Use: Large pot plant or hanging baskets
Height: 30 inches or more
Shape: Bushy to slightly trailing
Origin: South Africa
Light Requirements: Medium to high
Humidity Requirements: Medium
Temperature Requirements: Warm
Unique Characteristics: Dainty fern-like foliage with black fruit

The Asparagus Fern is a favorite florist plant, where the ferns are used in flower bouquets and corsages. It is also a very useful fern-like house plant with much more tolerance to the home environment than the true ferns.

It is a member of the genus *Asparagus* and grows in much the same environmental conditions as the Asparagus of the garden. It needs moisture, good drainage, and warm temperatures for best growth, and more light than any of the ferns.

The Asparagus Fern makes an ideal pot plant for southern or western exposures, but do not place it where it can be burned by the hot sun.

During the winter it will continue growing, though at a slower rate if it has plenty of light. Fern-type humidity will keep the plant looking better when the heat is on, but under normal house conditions it will still remain attractive.

SPRENGERI FERN
Asparagus densiflorus cv. 'Sprengeri'

Use: Pot plant or hanging basket
Height: 30 inches or more in height and length
Shape: Bushy
Origin: South Africa
Light Requirements: Moderate to high
Humidity Requirements: Moderate
Temperature Requirements: Warm in the summer and may be cooler in the winter
Unique Characteristics: Dense, easy to grow fern-like plant with orange-red fruit

The Sprengeri Fern is not nearly as fern-like as the Asparagus Fern; in fact, to me it is not very fern-like at all. Even so, it is a most worthwhile plant for the home.

The Sprengeri Fern makes a beautiful pot plant for inside tables or in plant groupings where the light is sufficient. It is also an excellent inside-outside plant. Outside, pots of the Sprengeri Fern do well on porches, patios, and decks. It is also beautiful as a hanging pot or basket.

The only problem I find with this plant is leaf drop when conditions change such as when the heat or air conditioning is turned on, and when it is brought inside for the winter. It will soon adjust, however, and the needle drop will stop.

Grow Sprengeri Fern as you would the Asparagus Fern, using the same soil and watering practices as for ferns in general, except let it get a bit drier between waterings.

❦ COMMON SOUTHERN FIG
Ficus carica

Use: Large tub plant
Height: Over 6 feet
Shape: Large bush or tree
Origin: The Mediterranean area
Light Requirements: High but not direct sun
Humidity Requirements: Moderate to high
Temperature Requirements: Cool to warm
Unique Characteristics: Heavy foliage and tree appearance

I have grown the Common Southern Fig inside more for the fun of it than for its beauty, as well as to quench my desire to have a fig tree which was not forever getting killed back during our cold Sweet Apple winters. Surprisingly it does quite well. If you ever let it get dry, all the leaves will drop off. But, on occasion, you might even get a fig or two.

It makes an attractive upright plant when grown as a bush or it may be trained into a tree by removing all but the main stem. It should have plenty of light but not direct sun and should be kept evenly warm without great drops in temperature at night.

Grow it in a peat-light mixture to which you have added additional peat moss and agricultural limestone. Keep it well-watered and away from cold windows which may trigger it into a dormant stage. Fertilize regularly with fish oil emulsion and a balanced house plant fertilizer.

❦ GOLD DUST AUCUBA
Aucuba japonica cv. 'Variegata'

Use: Bright foliage plant
Height: 3 feet or more inside
Shape: Upright
Origin: Asia

Light Requirements: Moderate
Humidity Requirements: Medium high
Temperature Requirements: Moderate
Unique Characteristics: Brightly-colored variegated leaves; may be cut and left in fresh water for many weeks

Perhaps you did not expect to see this garden friend in the house plant section, but it is a useful addition to indoor plantings and to our inside-outside plant list.

Do not place it in a bright sunny spot; if you do, the leaves will develop the same washed-out appearance so commonly found in Aucubas grown in too much sun outside.

Use your regular peat-light mixture and plant in a large tub for best results. Give it plenty of root space because this plant will grow large.

Since the leaves transpire rapidly in the low humidity of the house, you must water frequently, using the standard rules described so many times. Keep foliage misted or use a vaporizer when the heat or air conditioning is running.

Fertilize with a complete balanced soluble or liquid fertilizer. Increase the frequency and rate of application when new growth starts in the spring.

IVY AND IVY-LIKE PLANTS

There are many trailing and climbing plants which carry the name Ivy along with various descriptive names. These make up a wonderful group of house plants even though their individual needs may vary. They are listed here to aid in identification.

ENGLISH IVY
Hedera Helix and many cultivars

Use: Bush pot plant for its foliage, vine plant, and as cone and topiary plants
Height: Various, according to method of training
Shape: Various
Origin: Europe, West Asia, North Africa
Light Requirements: High
Humidity Requirements: Medium
Temperature Requirements: Moderate
Unique Characteristics: Easy to grow and very versatile in training

English Ivy is so common as a garden plant that it is seldom seriously considered as a house plant though it does quite well in an indoor setting.

I prefer several of the cultivars as house plants over the common English Ivy of the garden. With cv. 'Wilsonii,' my favorite, I have made some lovely plants trained on a wire cone frame inserted over an eight-inch pot. I have also made hanging baskets with this dainty-leaf cultivar.

Keep all English Ivy plants moist but not soggy, and well-fertilized, especially during active growth which comes most of the time. The addition of an organic fertilizer like fish oil emulsion in the fertilizing schedule is helpful.

GRAPE IVY
Cissus rhombifolia

Use: Trailing foliage plant
Height: 3 feet or more
Shape: Depends on method of training
Origin: Central to South America
Light Requirements: Moderate
Humidity Requirements: Moderate
Temperature Requirements: Cool to warm
Unique Characteristics: Easy to grow and will last for many years in the same pot

The Grape Ivy is one of those plants which seems to belong in my home. I like it and it likes me! In our early days in Sweet Apple we had one which was always beautiful. When we moved to Egypt it was lost in the shuffle. One of the first plants we bought upon our return was a Grape Ivy and it has survived ever since.

We grow our Grape Ivy in a large ten-inch azalea pot, and it has been replanted only once. The soil is a standard peat-light mixture, and we fertilize it with a regular soluble solution, adding fish oil emulsion on occasion. We water it when it seems to need it and otherwise leave it alone.

Our Grape Ivy sits on a plant stand on the screened porch in the summer and in the living room in the winter. My only problem has been when it gets the hot winter sun through the large picture window or if someone happens to open the heat vent near it. Then we lose a number of leaves quickly.

It can be just as successful for you if you watch the water and place it in the light but not in the direct sun.

SWEDISH IVY
Plectranthus nummularius

Use: Trailing pot plant or in hanging baskets
Height: Up to 36 inches in length
Shape: Trailing
Origin: South Africa
Light Requirements: Medium
Humidity Requirements: Moderate
Temperature Requirements: Cool to warm
Unique Characteristics: Easy to root and to grow; few problems

I always keep several hanging baskets filled with Swedish Ivy (sometimes called Creeping Charlie in the South) growing inside and outside during the summer. The waxy leaves are most attractive and the thick trailing plant makes an ideal hanging basket for porches and for a bright area inside.

It has few problems and grows well with a minimum of effort. If kept in a place where it is happy, it will last for years, needing attention only when it becomes too crowded in its pot or basket.

It may not be so happy when switching locations if the light conditions are different. I have found that those taken from outside to the indoors will drop many leaves and the new ones which come forth are much smaller and darker in color. The reverse is true when I take mine outside in the spring. I have overcome this problem by putting them in the greenhouse for the winter where the light conditions match those of the summer locations.

Swedish Ivy needs moist but not wet or soggy soil. A peat-light mixture is perfect and I let the soil dry out between waterings. You can tell when they are dry by the rather dull appearance of the foliage. A thorough watering will quickly restore the healthy look.

I fertilize mine all year, though I reduce the amount of water in the winter when growth is slow.

There are several other attractive members of this genus which may also be called Swedish Ivy. This one, *Plectranthus nummularius,* is the easiest to grow.

KALANCHOE or AIR PLANT
Kalanchoe pinnata

Use: Foliage and flowering pot plant
Height: 18 inches or more
Shape: Upright, bushy
Origin: Uncertain but widely adapted in the tropics
Light Requirements: High
Humidity Requirements: Medium
Temperature Requirements: Warm
Unique Characteristics: The leaves produce small plantlets on the edge which may be removed and potted for new plants.

The Kalanchoe is a real novelty because of its ability to produce new plants on the edges of the leaves. It is widely grown with fleeting success, especially when blossoms are the goal.

The main problem is that it requires a great deal of light and is most happy in direct sun, but it also cannot be placed next to a cold window for it has a low tolerance to cold night temperatures.

Grow Kalanchoe in a peat-light mixture to which you add one-third sand or perlite. Water when the surface of the soil in the pot is dry to the touch and fertilize moderately with a complete fertilizer.

MING ARALIA
Polyscias fruticosa cv. 'Elegans'

Use: Shrub-type plant
Height: 3 feet or more
Shape: Upright and graceful
Origin: India to Polynesia
Light Requirements: Medium to high

Ming Aralia

A Norfolk Isle Pine in Kuala Lumpur

The Ming Aralia grows thick and bushy when given warm temperatures and high humidity.

A large Norfolk Isle Pine in Kuantan, Malaysia

Humidity Requirements: Medium
Temperature Requirements: Warm
Unique Characteristics: The brown stems twist and turn and the leaves are gracefully cut.

Though the Ming Aralia is most attractive, it is not a beginner's plant because it is subject to spider mites and many growth problems. When carefully grown, however, it is worth the effort.

The twisting branches give it an oriental appearance which adds a unique dimension to plantings or groups of more common pot plants. In fact, it is often used as a bonsai plant.

Grow it in your regular peat-light mix and water when the surface of the soil in the pot is beginning to feel dry. Fertilize regularly with a complete house plant fertilizer.

The Ming Aralia should be grown in good light but never allowed to become chilled by being placed next to a window.

MOTHER-IN-LAW'S TONGUE or SNAKE PLANT
Sanseviera trifasciata

(See succulents)

NEPHTHYTIS or ARROWHEAD VINE
Syngonium podophyllum

Use: Potted vine
Height: 3 feet or more
Shape: Upright climber
Origin: Mexico to Panama
Light Requirements: Moderate to bright
Humidity Requirements: Moderate
Temperature Requirements: Warm
Unique Characteristics: Foliage is variegated when young but turns green when the plant is maturing

This is a popular house plant which takes relatively little care. It is best grown in a large pot where it can be trained to climb up a piece of bark wood.

Water when the soil surface is beginning to feel dry and fertilize during the growth period.

NORFOLK ISLAND PINE
Araucaria heterophylla

Use: Large tubbed tree
Height: Easily 6 feet or more

Shape: Upright tree form
Origin: Norfolk Island (between New Caledonia and New Zealand)
Light Requirements: High
Humidity Requirements: Medium
Temperature Requirements: Warm
Unique Characteristics: Its rank and file appearance and dark color

This exceptionally beautiful tree is grown outside in various warmer parts of the world. There are many growing outside in lower Florida. I have seen them growing beautifully in Egypt, the Caribbean, Kenya, the Philippines, Malaysia, and Indonesia. In fact, I suppose, everywhere a beautiful needle-foliaged tree is desired, one will find this gorgeous plant.

The most beautiful specimen I have ever seen was a 60-foot monster growing on Mindanao in the Philippines. We even had a small specimen in our yard in Kuala Lumpur, Malaysia.

Of course in our part of the world, the Norfolk Island Pine is grown as a pot or tub plant, for it can stand no frost. Most are grown in an eight- or twelve-inch pot where they are happy for a few years, perhaps. Then they must be repotted into a tub or they will gradually die. As a large tubbed plant they will last for many years, and when well cared for, they will add striking beauty to the inside of a home.

Use the regular peat-light mixture, and be sure that there is good drainage in the bottom of the pot or tub. Overwatering is disastrous, and so let the soil surface dry before waterings. When you water a large-tubbed Norfolk Island Pine, be sure to water enough each time. The roots become very heavy toward the center of the soil ball and it is necessary to slowly water down the stem. This will allow the water to move through the dense root ball and outward into the soil holding the feeder or white roots. Be sure that the entire soil area is moist every time you water but do not water too frequently.

These plants grow large and should be fertilized during their periods of active growth, which is generally from spring until fall. A monthly application of a complete fertilizer should be enough.

If spider mites are a problem, control them with a good house plant miticide.

PALMS

More than almost any other group of plants, palms give the feeling of a warm, tropical environment. When traveling south, our first indication of reaching the almost always warm part of our country is the sight of tall palms growing beside the road.

In the tropical zone, palms are abundant, and though not associated with jungles, they are certainly associated with ever-present warmth and the tropics. On my island of Guimaras, the Coconut Palm was an economic necessity. They were everywhere. Coconut Palms provided excellent wood for houses and furniture; food and drink; a source of income from copra; needed shade; and sturdy windbreaks offering protection from the monsoons. We even used the ground-up fiber of the husk as a substitute for peat moss.

In Malaysia, Oil Palm estates cover thousands and thousands of acres and stretch for mile after mile. They are the source of huge amounts of revenue for the country. Rattan, so popular as wood for furniture, is a palm which grows throughout Southeast Asia where I have spent so much time. Matted palm leaves are used for roofs and sides of houses as well as mats on which many sleep.

In the Middle East the Date Palm provides a delicious food from the fruit and material to make baskets from the mid-ribs of the leaves.

In all of my travels in the tropics, palms are seen as landscape plants, house plants, and patio or tub plants as well as economic plants. They are everywhere that people live. Our house in Kuala Lumpur had four different types of palms in the yard. My office had even more than that. As a landscape and garden plant, they are a staple.

On a trip home from Malaysia, I was horrified to hear from one authority that palms were out of vogue as a houseplant just when I was learning how wonderful these plants are and how easy they are to grow in pots, tubs, and planters. I had learned that there are so many more exquisite types than the few which our nursery growers provide, and I could not believe that they were no longer popular.

I hope that their popularity has not been diminished in your eyes, for palms certainly fit the bill as good house plants. Even the few which are available are most worthwhile and should be used inside whenever possible.

Palms are easy to grow provided they are grown under the proper conditions. Poorly-grown palms can be as ratty and unattractive as any plant with problems; a well-grown palm can be as satisfying and attractive a plant as you will ever grow.

Plant palms in soil that is light and high in humus. In general, they do best when the soil holds just enough moisture but is never soggy. Sogginess is deadly to almost all palms and certainly to those commonly used as house plants. The ideal soil is a peat-light mixture to which is added perlite or sand and dehydrated cattle manure.

Keep palms evenly watered as they are in constant need of moisture. Don't overwater. When the surface of the soil is barely damp to the touch, water thoroughly, allowing the water to soak into the ball of earth at the stem and work outward. Never let the soil separate from the sides of the pot for then the ball is much too dry for their liking.

Most palms grown indoors do best in good light but not in direct sun. Hot sunlight through a window can be particularly harmful. The best temperature range is on the warm side, especially at night, which is another reason to keep them away from windows, which tend to be colder than the room on winter nights.

Fertilize year-round with greater concentrations in the solution during the spring and summer and less in the fall and winter.

Palms, unlike most plants, should be repotted when in active growth rather than when semidormant during the fall and winter. The roots need to regenerate immediately after repotting and the plants must be in active growth for this regeneration to occur.

Spider mites and mealybugs are their main insect problems and should be controlled as soon as discovered. Take infested plants outside, if possible, and wash off the insects with a strong spray of clear water. Let dry and then spray

Palms are some of the most beautiful of tropical plants.

The Oil Palm provides vegetable oil for much of the world.

Don Hastings III enjoys young coconut water.

The nut of the Oil Palm

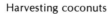

Harvesting coconuts

A Chinese fan palm

The rattan before stripping of sharp spines

Rattan for furniture comes from this palm.

The beautiful and useful golden coconut

A new coconut palm on a beach in Malaysia

An accented palm with Ti plants

Sealing Wax palm in Kuala Lumpur

Palms are a landscaper's delight in the tropics.

Areca Palms grow well in a home

The unusual Traveler's Palm

An Areca Palm in a landscape setting

with an insecticidal soap. Mealybugs may be difficult to wash off but can be killed by touching each one with denatured alcohol on a cotton swab.

If leaf spot diseases occur on occasion, they are most often the result of dusty leaves, too much sun through a window, and poor growth in general.

The older leaves of palms, especially at the bottom, often lose their function and die. This general deterioration is natural and is seen in nature all the time. Merely cut off the offending leaf and all will be well. However, if they begin to brown back from the ends, you probably have a root or water problem which may be caused by:

- Too much water
- Too little water
- Too small a container; needs repotting
- Too heavy and poorly-drained soil mixture
- Growing in too cold a spot
- Growing in a hot, bright, sunny window
- Presence of sowbugs or pillbugs in the ball of earth

The list of palms to grow is too often restricted to those available in plant shops. This is a great pity, and so always be on the lookout for new ones in plant shops which cater to those interested in better cultivars of all houseplants.

The most often found palms are:
- Areca Palm
- Fishtail Palm
- Lady Palm
- Miniature Date Palm
- Parlor Palm (often referred to as Neanthe bella).

ARECA PALM
Chrysalidocarpus lutescens

Origin: Madagascar

The Areca Palm is one of the easier palms to grow inside. It may be trained into a single stalk palm tree or it may be allowed to form a bushy clump, which is the way it generally grows outside in tropical gardens.

Inside our homes it does best in diffused light but will suffer in direct sun or too little light. Watch your water and do not let the soil surface dry between waterings, especially in the spring and summer when it is actively growing.

FISHTAIL PALM
Caryota mitis

Origin: Burma, Malay Peninsula, Java, Philippines

This is not a beginner's palm but one for the devotee of exotic indoor decorative material. It is found surprisingly often in plant shops despite its temperamental ways. It needs bright light but not direct sun, and even watering. A humidifier close by will help tremendously to keep it healthy.

The Queen Palm is rarely found in our plant shops.

Fishtail palm in an atrium

Fishtail Palm growing outside in Malaysia

The Lady Palm used in a planter

The Lady Palm has larger leaves in the tropics, where the humidity is high.

Once you get the hang of growing this palm, you will have a longtime friend for it grows well in a tub and will last for years.

It has a tendency to send up shoots from the base and may be grown as a clump palm or as a single-stem tree.

LADY PALM
Rhapis excelsa

Origin: Southern China

There are a number of fan palms which are widely grown in pots and tubs in tropical homes and gardens. The Lady Palm is certainly an easy one to grow and will do as well inside for us as in the tropics. Lady Palm grows in a clump with bamboo-like stalks from which the fan leaves arise and form a beautiful rounded plant. It grows slowly and will last for several years in a proper size pot.

It is one of the easiest of all palms to grow, provided it is not placed in too much light nor planted in too heavy soil. Keep soil on the damp side all the time but do not keep too wet. Improper watering will cause the leaflets to die back from the tip and become unsightly.

MINIATURE DATE PALM
Phoenix Roebelenii

Origin: Laos

The Miniature Date Palm is one of our most elegant house plants. It is a relatively dwarf plant with long, very dark green, fern-like leaves. Small plants are excellent as table plants while larger ones are attractive as low, bushy floor plants.

It will take less light than many other palms and will survive in a dimly lit room. It does best in higher than average household humidity, and so keep it misted or place a humidifier nearby.

PARLOR PALM or NEANTHE BELLA PALM
Chamaedorea elegans

Origin: Mexico, Guatemala

The Parlor Palm (often called by the incorrect botanical name of Neanthe bella) is said to be one of the most widely grown house plants in the United States. It is a beginner's plant for, unlike most palms, it takes very low light and may grow in drier soil and with poorer watering practices. This in no way means you should be casual about its culture. All plants do best when tended properly and this is no exception.

If you treat it like other palms, it will reach a height of five or six feet and be a beautiful addition to your home.

OTHER PALMS

There are many others which are certainly as outstanding and easily grown as these and worth having when you run across them at a plant shop.

Neanthe Bella Palm growing in Kuala Lumpur

A potted Neanthe Bella Palm

The bright fruit of the Macarthur Palm

The beautiful Macarthur Palm
growing in Kuala Lumpur

A huge Fan Palm

Spectacular red of the Sealing Wax Palm
leaf

Sealing Wax Palm

Bottle Palm

The following palms are those which I have observed in the places where I have lived or frequented in the tropics and which are used as potted plants inside and outside in those places. I hope that you will be able to find a few of these more exotic ones to try out.

CHINESE FAN PALM
Livistona chinensis

Origin: China

There are a number of fan palms which you see planted in pots and tubs. The Chinese Fan Palm, sometimes called Chinese Fountain Palm, is one of the more beautiful. It does become a bit overpowering when it grows large and arches outward with long-leaf stalks. In the right place it is a beautiful addition to a home.

Be careful, however, to keep it out of direct sun because the fan palms look ratty when the leaves develop brown tips.

MacARTHUR PALM
Ptychosperma Macarthurii

Origin: New Guinea

The MacArthur Palm is common in Malaysia and the Philippines as a hedge-type plant, yard specimen, planter box plant, and pot plant. You see them in gardens, patios, covered outdoor living areas, and indoors.

It will take a great deal of light but try not to put it in a hot window, where it could also be too cold during the winter's nights. Keep the humidity higher than normal and water as you do other palms. It is a relatively heavy feeder during periods of growth.

I like the MacArthur Palm when grown with two or three stalks. These are jointed, somewhat like bamboo, and they are most attractive.

The ones in my yard in Kuala Lumpur bore long clusters of brightly colored fruits but I would doubt seeing these when growing it inside our home in Sweet Apple.

The MacArthur Palm is considered one of the most satisfactory and beautiful palms to be grown as a house or pot plant. It has a reputation for being of easy culture and for its good performance even with little care.

SEALING WAX PALM
Cyrostachys Lakka, C. Renda

Origin: Malay Peninsula, Sumatra, Borneo

I had never seen the Sealing Wax Palm until I went to Singapore the first time. This extremely handsome palm is grown widely as a garden ornamental and tub plant for homes. In Malaysia you often see streets lined with them.

It is unique in having bright red stems along with beautiful green, fern-type palm leaves. Most of the time it is grown in clumps, but on rare occasions you will see one which stands as a single-trunk palm. There, the red trunk stands out like a beacon. I was overwhelmed when I saw it for the first time.

They are widely grown inside, even in air-conditioned homes, and it escapes me as to why they have not been popularized by growers of house plants here.

The reason may be that they may require more light than many of our homes have. However, nurserymen in the tropics insist that they will do as well as most other palms grown as house plants in the States.

SPECIALTY PALMS

There are a huge number of palms which may eventually find their way into commercial production. As they are found in house plant outlets, you should try those which fit your decorative plans. Grow each new one as I have indicated for palms in general, changing your techniques when specific notes are given at the plant shop.

BOTTLE PALM or PONYTAIL PALM
Beaucarnea recurvata

This is a small-growing palm with weeping leaves and a trunk with an enlarged, bottle-shaped base.

SAGO PALM
Cycas revoluta

The Sago Palm is dense and grows extremely slowly. It makes a large trunk from which the palm leaves arise from short nodes (spacings). It is not for every home but fits well where a stiff palm is needed.

PEPEROMIA
Peperomia obtusifolia

Use: Table foliage plant
Height: 6 to 12 inches
Shape: Bushy
Origin: Tropical America and South Florida
Light Requirements: Bright but not direct sun
Humidity Requirements: Moderate
Temperature Requirements: Warm
Unique Characteristics: Unusual crinkly foliage ('Emerald Ripple' is a particularly attractive cultivar.)

The Peperomias are very fine table plants—relatively easy to grow and trouble-free. Water when the surface of the soil becomes dry to the touch and fertilize when in growth.

PHILODENDRONS

There are a number of plants which have been known from time to time as Philodendrons though they may have been discovered to be taxonomically separate from the genus Philodendron. These are listed below and they take similar growing conditions, which are as follows:

Most Philodendrons and Philodendron-type plants are native to the humid tropical forests and should be treated accordingly. They do best in loose, well-drained soil and warm temperatures. In the home, they are best grown in low to moderate light, average to high humidity, and warm temperatures. Though they require moisture, they should never be in soggy soil. Root rot is often a severe problem when the soil is kept too wet. Remember the lesson I learned while farming in the jungle: the soil where jungle plants thrive is seldom if ever soggy and water-laden. It drains quickly and dries out between the monsoon-type downpours. Jungle soil is loose and porous, much like the peat-light soil mixes which I have recommended over and over for use with tropical house plants.

Fertilizing schedules with a complete balanced fertilizer should follow the growth of the plant. The addition of an organic fertilizer such as Fish Oil Emulsion is helpful.

There are few pests which attack these plants. Mealybugs are perhaps the worst. Remove the culprits with a cotton swab dipped in alcohol and spray with a good house plant insecticide.

GOLDEN POTHOS
Epipremnum aureum

Use: Climbing vine
Height: Size is limited by growing conditions
Shape: Upright vine
Origin: Asia
Light Requirements: Moderate but not in direct sun
Humidity Requirements: Medium
Temperature Requirements: Warm
Unique Characteristics: Vigorous climbing vine with several leaf forms depending on maturity

The Golden Pothos is one of the most attractive of all the native climbing vines that I saw in Southeast Asia. There was an especially beautiful one climbing to the high branches of a tree at the place where I stayed on my regular visits to our project. The place faced east out to the South China Sea and when the sun rose, it shone on this Golden Pothos which reached up to over fifty feet. The golden early morning sun shining on the Golden Pothos' brightly colored leaves accentuated its beauty.

In the home, the Golden Pothos does quite well. You can purchase young plants which still have their smaller juvenile foliage. These may be used as small pot plants. The larger potted plants which have developed their mature foliage make handsome tub specimens to grow on a bark slab or pole.

Golden Pothos climbing a tree in Malaysia

Adult leaves of the Golden Pothos are rarely seen inside.

Golden Pothos as a potted houseplant has smaller juvenile leaves.

Very juvenile leaves of Golden Pothos may not be as variegated as are the large adult leaves.

Heartleaf Philodendron growing on a coconut tree

A mature Heartleaf Philodendron in Green Park, Makati, Philippines

Spadeleaf Philodendron

Spadeleaf Philodendron growing in Green Park, Makati, Philippines

Splitleaf Philodendron growing in a tree in Malaysia

Grow the Golden Pothos in a standard peat-light mixture. Water well when the surface of the soil in the pot is dry to the touch. Do not overwater. Fertilize on a regular schedule, but increase the amount when it is actively growing.

There are many cultivars from which to choose.

HEART-LEAF PHILODENDRON
Philodendron scandens subspecies *oxycardium* and *P. cordatum*

Use: Indoor climbing or trailing vine
Height: 4 feet or more
Shape: Vine
Origin: Tropical America
Light Requirements: Low to medium
Humidity Requirements: Medium
Temperature Requirements: Moderate
Unique Characteristics: Very easy to grow inside and tolerates low light

The Heart-leaf Philodendron is the first indoor plant that many people obtain. It grows easily with a minimum of effort and the most casual care. It will remain an attractive plant for years.

Most new indoor gardeners will leave it in the plant shop pot for much too long. Though it will continue to grow under these adverse conditions, the plant may soon get weak. For this reason, I like to shift the plant into a larger pot when I bring it home even if it looks a little lost for a while. The reason is that it is most often used as a climbing plant and it becomes rather difficult to repot when it has twined around some permanent fixture in the house.

If grown in too dark a place, the nodes will elongate and it appears very stemmy and less attractive. Also, a lack of water and lack of regular fertilizing will cause it to become "leggy" with most of the leaves on the top one-third of the vine.

The Heart-leaf Philodendron may be pruned back and repotted when it becomes unattractive. The prunings will easily root (even in water) and you can get new plants.

SPADE LEAF PHILODENDRON
Philodendron domesticum

The Spade Leaf Philodendron is similar in culture and use to the Heart-leaf Philodendron. The leaves are larger and shaped like a spade instead of a heart. It is less viny and slower in growth due to the larger leaves. There are several cultivars but one of the most interesting is the green-leaf, red-stem 'Red Princess.'

SPLIT LEAF PHILODENDRON
Monstera deliciosa

Use: Large potted or tubbed plant
Height: 3 feet or over
Shape: Upward-spreading

Origin: Central America
Light Requirements: Moderate
Humidity Requirements: Medium
Temperature Requirements: Warm
Unique Characteristics: Large-growing, vase-shaped plant which has large leaves
   with perforations and splits

The Split Leaf Philodendron is one of the standard large pot or tub plants for the home. It is much prized and often grown for its unusual tropical appearance and heavy texture. It is excellent as a large tub plant to sit on the floor and give a heavy accent to a room. Be sure to give this plant ample support with something like a heavy bark slab.

Use the standard culture for Philodendrons. The only additional advice is to mist the leaves upon occasion and to keep the large leaves clean by wiping with a soapy solution and rinsing thoroughly. Yellow leaves will often appear at the base of the leaf stem and should be removed.

TREE PHILODENDRON
Philodendron Selloum

Use: Large pot plant
Height: 3 feet or more
Shape: Upright
Origin: Southern Brazil
Light Requirements: Medium
Humidity Requirements: Moderate to high
Temperature Requirements: Warm
Unique Characteristics: Large attractive leaves and upright habit

The Tree Philodendron, like the Split Leaf Philodendron, is most common in indoor gardening. It is an excellent plant for large pots or tubs and is widely used as a floor accent plant. Smaller plants are commonly grown in six- or eight-inch pots, but they soon outgrow the space and have to be shifted to a larger container.

The Tree Philodendron takes a similar culture to the others listed before.

PICKABACK PLANT
Tolmiea Menziesii

Use: For pots or hanging baskets
Height: 12 inches or more
Shape: Bushy
Origin: Western North America
Light Requirements: Moderate
Humidity Requirements: Medium
Temperature Requirements: Cool to warm
Unique Characteristics: It reproduces by sprouting a new plant at the base of a
   leaf. It is easy to start new plants from these babies.

We have grown Pickabacks (we call them Piggyback Plants) for many years, and at one time Betsy had so many "youngsters" that she sold them commercially. She would take some of the leaves with the small new plants from the mother plant and remove about one-half of the leaf surrounding the baby plant. Her trick was to leave a portion of the stem of the leaf so that she could anchor the baby into the soil in a regular seed flat. As soon as the youngsters were growing, she would pot them in four- or five-inch pots for sale.

Pickaback Plants grow best in a peat-light mixture which drains well. They do not like overwatering. It is best to let them dry a bit before watering again, but be careful because they will wilt quickly when the soil is too dry. This may scare you, but simply soak the pot thoroughly and soon the plant will be back to normal.

We grow ours in large pots and in hanging pots and baskets both indoors and on the porches. I fertilize them at least once a month throughout the year, for they seem to grow all the time when they are inside the house.

Pickaback Plants may be planted directly in the ground in rock gardens or shady spots, but they will not stand our winter cold. Since they are so easy to propagate, they may be used as an annual.

The only serious pest is the spider mite which can devastate plants if not controlled with a good miticide. Watch for these pests for they can grow out of control very quickly and ruin a beautiful plant in no time. The foliage will appear dull and gray when the spider mite is really active.

PODOCARPUS or SOUTHERN YEW
Podocarpus macrophyllus Maki

Use: Pot or tub plant
Height: 4 feet or more
Shape: Upright bush
Origin: China
Light Requirements: Maximum
Humidity Requirements: Moderate
Temperature Requirements: Cool
Unique Characteristics: A beautiful needle plant with heavy, upright growth

Podocarpus is well known to Southern gardeners as an excellent outdoor plant for much of the South. It is seldom thought of as a houseplant, for we are too accustomed to seeing it growing in the garden. However, it does very nicely in a pot while still small and in a tub as it grows older.

Grow Podocarpus in a pot large enough to keep it growing for at least a year. A small four- or six-inch nursery-grown container plant should be shifted to an eight- or ten-inch pot when you take it home. Use a regular peat-light mixture.

Larger plants may be replanted in sixteen- or eighteen-inch tubs where they will last for many years.

Podocarpus is easy to grow inside if the atmosphere is not too dry and if there is plenty of light. It may be pruned into an upright column or may be tipped so that it is bushy.

❧ PRAYER PLANT
Maranta leuconeura Kerchoviana

Use: Interesting table plant
Height: 8 inches
Shape: Upright to spreading
Origin: Tropical America
Light Requirements: Medium with no direct sun
Humidity Requirements: High
Temperature Requirements: Warm
Unique Characteristics: The leaves turn inward and stand upright at night.

I have never been really successful with the Prayer Plant since its treatment differs from my other plants. This is quite a bother, especially in the greenhouse where all plants in the house are watered at one time. It always seems to be either too wet or too dry and soon looks horrible. However, friends have them and are quite adept at keeping them beautiful. Perhaps it just wears my patience too thin.

My best results have been when growing the Prayer Plant in my regular peat-light mix and keeping it in a cool bright spot in the house.

❧ RUBBER PLANT
Ficus elastica cv. 'Decora'

Use: Large table plant or tubbed for a large tree
Height: 6 feet or more
Shape: Tree form
Origin: Nepal, India, and Burma
Light Requirements: Bright
Humidity Requirements: Moderate
Temperature Requirements: Warm
Unique Characteristics: The large decorative leaves and glossy sheen

This is not the noted commercial rubber tree (*Hevea brasiliensis*), but is a prized ornamental plant throughout much of Asia. It is now used throughout the world as a garden plant where there is no frost and as an indoor plant elsewhere. Huge plants grow as trees along the streets of Cairo, and in the Philippines and Malaysia they are everywhere. It is one of the really beautiful decorative plants of the world.

The Rubber Plant is not of difficult culture, provided the soil is loose and well-drained and it is planted in a pot large enough to allow it to keep growing. Most of the complaints about this plant are that it grows too tall and gets out of bounds. It should never be tipped to restrict its upward growth for that ruins its tree shape. However, if it is grown in bright light and not given too much fertilizer, side shoots may develop. This will slow down the upright growth and allow the plant to adopt a spreading growth pattern.

Watch your watering practices. Always water thoroughly, allowing the water to run down the base of the stem and seep from the center of the root ball outward.

Pickaback Plant

The common Ficus elastica 'Decora' found in the tropical landscape is also a wonderful houseplant.

Variegated Ficus elastica

Screw Pine, Pandanus in Malaysia

Fruit of the Screw Pine, Pandanus

Water when the soil surface begins to feel dry to the touch. Too much water will cause a root problem and the plant will seldom perform satisfactorily.

Do not be alarmed when the lower leaves begin to yellow and fall off. This is natural and means that the plant will soon begin an upward spurt of growth. When this happens, apply fertilizer. If the yellowing spreads upward and there are only a few leaves at the top, your plant may be receiving too much (or on rare occasions, too little) water or may be suffering from too little light or too low humidity.

Keep the large leaves free from dust and house grime. Use a warm soapy solution to clean them and then rinse off the soapy residue.

A variegated form of the Rubber Plant has received quite a bit of publicity. However, I much prefer the green form because of the beautiful glossy leaves.

❧ SCREW PINE
Pandanus sp. most often *P. Veitchii*

Use: Table plant when young, floor when older
Height: May reach 5 feet
Shape: Upright tree shape
Origin: Orient and Polynesia
Light Requirements: High but not direct sun
Humidity Requirements: Medium to high
Temperature Requirements: Warm
Unique Characteristics: Tough, coarse-growing plant with heavy spines on the margins of the leaves

The first natural Pandanus I ever saw was in a planting near the beach on the east coast of Malaysia. There, a young lad was trying to introduce me to the native language, Bahasa Malaysia, and we were making every effort to "commonize" on words of English and comparable words of Bahasa. I pointed at a strange tree and asked what it was. His reply was pokok (pronounced po'ko). Much later I found that the word meant tree and was not the name of the plant which eventually I found was the native Screw Pine. In its natural, mature state its leaves are used for thatching and little else, certainly not for decorative plants. Growing wild, the leaves are as armed as a Yucca and as dangerous if one tries to pass through a thicket of Pandanus.

Once home again, I found the Pandanus, in its juvenile state, to be a readily accepted houseplant. It is easy to grow and will withstand the awful conditions which most of our houses give to plants. Pot it in our regular, well-drained mixture; fertilize it regularly when growing in the summer; let it dry between waterings, and you will have a delightful plant for your house. Watch out, however; the older spines will cut you, just like a Yucca.

❧ SHAMROCK
Oxalis Acetosella, Oxalis purpurea and *Trifolium* sp.

Use: Table plant
Height: 8 to 10 inches

Shape: Bushy
Origin: Europe
Light Requirements: Medium
Humidity Requirements: Medium to high
Temperature Requirements: Cool
Unique Characteristics: Attractive foliage and white or rose pink flowers

I always hesitate writing about the Shamrock for it is said that the world is divided into two parts: those who claim that the Irish Shamrock is a clover and those who claim it is an Oxalis. From all I have read, it is probably a clover, but commerce says it is the nice pot plant which is an Oxalis. In fact there are several Oxalis which are used as a Shamrock. The one that I write about and that I think is the best for a house plant is the *Oxalis Acetosella,* a bulbous plant with attractive white flowers.

I have grown this latter plant for many years, and it is one of our favorite living room table plants. We grow it on a table near the window but back far enough for the plant to get plenty of light, but no direct sun. In the winter it stays rather cool and is far enough from the heat vent not to suffer from the warm dry air.

I grow this plant in my regular peat-light mixture and keep it moderately fertilized with applications whenever it is growing and do not fertilize when it is resting.

This plant has a definite growth cycle which you must understand so that you won't throw away a perfectly good plant. It grows profusely, blooms, and then seems to die away. Instead of dying, however, it is beginning to rest. At this time, reduce the frequency of watering and stop fertilizing. Place it in a cool spot for about a month. Then bring it back into the light, fertilize it, and water it. Soon a whole new cycle of growth and bloom will come.

These Shamrocks are subject to spider mites which you should control or your plant will suffer tremendously.

SCHEFFLERA
Brassaia actinophylla

Use: Potted or tubbed shrub or tree
Height: 6 feet or more
Shape: Bush or tree
Origin: S.E. Asia to Australia and Hawaii
Light Requirements: Moderate
Humidity Requirements: Medium
Temperature Requirements: Warm
Unique Characteristics: Tough, large growing plant

Scheffleras are almost universally grown as tropical or house plants. I found huge Schefflera trees beside the Nile in Cairo. They were widely grown in the Philippines and even more numerous in Malaysia. In all these places, I saw them in pots as well as in the garden soil.

Here in the South, they are one of the most widely grown of all house plants because of their stunning shape and foliage and ease of culture. The only thing

Arborcola, a dwarf Schefflera

Shamrock

Arborcola is an excellent tub plant

A Schefflera growing in Egypt

191

which seems to destroy a Schefflera is poorly-drained soil and too much water. Use a peat-light mixture and follow the principles set forth for most tropicals, except allow the potting soil to dry down before watering again.

A dwarf form is designated, erroneously it seems, as Schefflera arborcola. These are also widely grown. There was a beautiful planting outside my office in Kuala Lumpur, and I have seen them in many tropical countries. Since they are commonly found under that name, ask for them as arborcolas and you will be on the right track.

❧ SPIDER PLANT
Chlorophytum comosum

Use: Table or hanging basket plant
Height: 12 to 15 inches
Shape: Trailing or spreading
Origin: South Africa
Light Requirements: Medium
Humidity Requirements: Medium
Temperature Requirements: Warm
Unique Characteristics: It produces new plants at the end of wiry stems. There are both green and variegated forms.

I have enjoyed growing the Spider Plant for many years. We have a beautiful one hanging over our kitchen table. There are several on our porch and more in hanging pots on the porch during the summer. It is easy to grow and easy to propagate.

Plant a small Spider Plant in almost any kind of pot using a regular peat-light mixture, and it will be happy and grow well for you. It thrives on abuse, being much happier when underwatered than overwatered. Monthly liquid fertilizing keeps it healthy.

I live in the country where my delicious water comes from a deep well, and so I do not have the problem city dwellers have with chlorinated, fluoridated water which is very harmful to the Spider Plant, especially the variegated form.

My less fortunate city friends tell me that one should place fluoridated and chlorinated tap water in a shallow pan and leave it on the kitchen cabinet overnight before using it as water for the plant. This allows the harmful gases to escape. I think that boiling the water for twenty minutes and cooling in a shallow pan overnight would be even better.

No matter which method you use, removing these gases is important if you are going to have beautiful Spider Plants, unless you are really smart and move to the country where the water is pure and the air is magnificent!

Propagating Spider Plants is almost as much fun as growing them. After they reach some age, you will notice long, wiry shoots arching outward and downward. At the end of these shoots you will soon see a new little Spider Plant. Pinch the little feller off and press him into a pot filled with our peat-light mixture and soon you will have a beautiful new plant.

SUCCULENTS

All cacti are succulents, but all succulents are not cacti. This is a fact we should all remember. A number of plants for the inside fall into the succulent class, only some of which are cactus.

Many succulents make excellent houseplants, though I must admit that they are certainly not my ideal for a plant to grow inside. Perhaps this is due to the years I spent in the inhospitable Sahara Desert of Egypt, or perhaps my lack of knowledge of these plants, but nonetheless they are not my favorites. Though their presence in my home doesn't inspire me, many devotees of these plants do wonders with them inside and proudly proclaim their worth.

They seem to thrive in lower humidity than the tropical plants which make up the greatest number of plants that we grow inside and the ones that I really enjoy. The main considerations for growing succulents are the soil and the light. They are mainly desert plants with very sparse roots. Excess moisture is detrimental and will quickly ruin most of these plants. A special "cactus mix" is best. I like to use my regular peat-light mixture to which is added one part sand and one part perlite. The formula follows:

- 2 parts regular peat-light mixture
- 1 part sand
- 1 part pure perlite

Light requirements are also different from those of our jungle plants in most but not all cases. Most but not all succulents are native to desert areas where bright sun is the rule. Place these in the brightest spots of the home. They should not, however, be in a west window where hot burning sun beams in. There are a few succulents of the forest and they can tolerate dimmer light.

Your local botanical garden or plant shop will have good information about types of succulents suitable for the home. In a few cities you might find good societies that specialize in these interesting plants and that will offer information on types and culture.

The following is a list of succulents that I have grown or am familiar with. The list is certainly not very extensive, but it is a good place to start your introduction to this fine group of plants.

❦ ALOE or BURN PLANT
Aloe barbadensis

Use: Medicinal pot plant for kitchen or table
Height: Eventually, 2 feet
Shape: Vase
Origin: Mediterranean area
Light Requirements: Medium
Humidity Requirements: Low
Temperature Requirements: Cool to warm
Unique Characteristics: Leaves contain a juice helpful against burns

Aloe Vera sits on Betsy Hastings' kitchen sink ready to soothe a kitchen burn.

Christmas Cactus that blossoms every Christmas.

Christmas Cactus

Green and Variegated Spider Plants with St. Fiacre at Floweracres

Green Spider Plant

The Aloe is an exception to my lack of fondness for succulents. I am partial to this plant, which Betsy and I have grown for many years with considerable success. One or two have reached enormous size and have provided many new plants. I think it most attractive and its needs are not nearly as demanding as many others in its group. I use my regular peat-light mixture and keep this plant on the dry side. No other problems are evident, high light not even being as critical as one might suppose.

Our kitchen always contains an Aloe Plant. It is easy to grow, and it is quickly available when Betsy needs to touch a scald or burn from cooking. When any of us receives one of these painful wounds, she quickly breaks a leaf off our kitchen Aloe and rubs the juice on the burn. As if by a miracle, the burning sensation disappears and the household returns to normal. Betsy has given leaves of her kitchen Aloe to neighbors with severe farming burns which were unhealed by pharmacy ointments, and they began to feel better almost immediately.

The wonderful thing about our kitchen Aloe is that it grows happily with virtually no light except that from the cabinet fluorescent tube under which it awaits a call to heal. Betsy waters it upon occasion and feeds it when there is any fertilizer left after her rounds with our houseplants. It seems to grow quite well.

I grow Aloes in my greenhouse to have available for all who want them. My son Chris even ventured briefly into the production of Aloe Plants for sale. Though hardly worthwhile commercially, he managed to help many people through their burns and scrapes.

Chris and I grow Aloes with another purpose in the greenhouse. We first take the side shoots and root them in the perlite rooting bed. We then pot them in a good mixture, watch our watering, fertilize monthly, and make them grow extravagantly. Some, we shift to 12- or 14-inch pots, and they become enormous, like the desert cactus which I have seen in central Mexico.

No matter how you propose to use Aloe, you will find this fabulous plant attractive and worthwhile. As Betsy says, "No home or kitchen should be without a pot of Aloe."

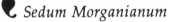 BURRO TAIL
Sedum Morganianum

Use: Foliage plant for tall pots or hanging baskets
Height: 2 to 3 feet
Shape: Trailing
Origin: Mexico
Light Requirements: Bright light
Humidity Requirements: Low
Temperature Requirements: Warm
Unique Characteristics: The unusual teardrop leaves are massed along the trailing stems. The color is an attractive silver-blue.

The Burro Tail is fun to grow for its unusual foliage and trailing habit. It may also blossom upon occasion, though the clusters of pink flowers are not the really significant attraction of the plant.

It is best grown in a peat-light mixture to which has been added generous amounts of sand, or in a cactus mixture. It is otherwise easy to grow provided it is given plenty of bright light and never overwatered or grown with plants that need high humidity. It is ideally suited to a bright sunny spot in normal house humidity.

CHRISTMAS CACTUS
Schlumbergera Bridgesii

Use: Table plant
Height: 12 to 18 inches, height and breadth
Shape: Arching upward and outward
Origin: Brazil
Light Requirements: Moderate to high
Humidity Requirements: Low to medium
Temperature Requirements: Cool in winter, warm in summer
Unique Characteristics: Bright cerise to red flowers in the late fall and winter

I was extremely impressed by my mother's ability always to have a beautiful Christmas Cactus in bloom for her annual Christmas party. I could never do that.

As I have mentioned, I have always admired Kathy Henderson's abilities when it comes to herbaceous plant materials including house plants. My deep feeling for Kathy as a person and horticulturist was intensified when I found out that her mother, also, had beautiful blooming Christmas Cactus each Christmas time. Kathy couldn't make hers bloom that well either!

She and I have discussed the procedure *ad infinitum* and recommended to our audiences to dry off the plants in September, put them in a dimly-lit place and hold them until early November. Then, water and fertilize lightly. Soon, she and I said, the pink buds would appear and be in bloom for Christmas. That is the way it should happen. However, that is not the way her mother and my mother did it. We still do not know how they managed, for the secret went with them. I don't achieve those results, and neither does Kathy. Perhaps we are just of the wrong generation, but maybe you can find your key to fantastic Christmas Cactus blooms at Christmas. It is surely worth a try; I shall never forget my mother's huge Christmas Cactus by the Sillibub bowl during the holiday season.

Off season and out of bloom, the Christmas Cactus is quite attractive as a table plant. I suppose one would not grow it just for foliage but it is certainly a good addition to your indoor plant collection whether in or out of bloom.

DESERT ROSE
Adenium obesum

Use: Table or floor plant
Height: 3 feet, height and breadth

Shape: Vase to upward spreading
Origin: Africa and desert Arabia
Light Requirements: High
Humidity Requirements: Medium to low
Temperature Requirements: Cool in winter, warm in summer
Unique Characteristics: Heavy succulent with huge flowers; sap contains a poison.

The Desert Rose is seldom seen in this country but is widely grown as a house plant in many countries. The first one I saw used as a house plant was in a friend's home in Singapore. In that part of the world, they are commonly grown as pot plants and sometimes in the ground in a dry part of the garden.

Grow them in a very loose, dry cactus mix and never overwater them. Give the Desert Rose as much sun as possible and set it outside during the warm seasons, under an eave of the house or in a bright spot on a porch where the summer rains will not keep it too wet. In Singapore, where it feels as though you could wring water out of the high-humidity air, it is quite happy. So with the proper soil you should be able to grow it without too much trouble. It is a succulent that will add a great deal to your collection of succulent plants.

JADE PLANT
Crassula argentea

Use: Table plant
Height: 36 inches or more
Shape: Bushy
Origin: Africa
Light Requirements: High
Humidity Requirements: Medium to low
Temperature Requirements: Cool in winter, warm in summer
Unique Characteristics: Heavy succulent with flowers when old

Memories of youth are often deceiving, but I am still convinced that the most beautiful Jade Plant I have ever seen was grown by the wife of our wonderful nursery superintendent, J. Wesley Watts. Mrs. Watts had this phenomenal plant in a huge clay pot on the porch of her house. In the winter, she placed the plant in an unheated room, and there it thrived. As a youngster, I would stand in awe of it, for never before or since have I seen such a monstrous Jade Plant in a home environment.

Mrs. Watts seemed to have the secret. When it is not growing, leave it alone, water it sparingly, and give it plenty of light through a window. My Jade Plants have never been as beautiful. Perhaps the central heat of our house in the winter is too dry and warm; perhaps we pamper it too much. Whatever the reason, Mrs. Watts had the secret, and I do not.

I have been moderately successful with Jade Plants but never as successful as she. My success comes from plenty of light, keeping the plant drier in the winter, and letting it grow in the summer with good watering and fertilizing.

Desert Rose

Desert Rose, a popular succulent houseplant in the Orient

A Ti Plant in bloom in the Philippines

Ti Plant in Kuala Lumpur

Ti Plant used in a mass planting in Malaysia

Too much water will cause the leaves to drop and the stems to become soft and rot. Too little water causes leaf drop. Growing a Jade Plant is a balance which tests a gardener's ability.

It is worth a try, however, for if you grow one half as well as Mrs. Watts or about as well as I, you will have a houseplant that will be a real bonus to your indoor plants.

OTHER SUCCULENTS

There are many other succulents which are suitable as house plants. The Agaves, other Aloes, and many cacti have been grown quite successfully inside. There are even cacti which have been grafted with one or more additional species on a single plant.

Devotees of this group of plants have joined together in societies which promote the use of succulents, especially cacti, inside the home. You may wish to expand your plantings by conferring with members of these societies or even joining with them and becoming a specialist in the art of growing these interesting plants.

TI PLANT or GOOD LUCK PLANT
Cordyline terminalis

Use: Upright pot or tub plant
Height: 3 feet or more
Shape: Upright
Origin: East Asia
Light Requirements: Moderate
Humidity Requirements: Medium
Temperature Requirements: Warm
Unique Characteristics: Easy to grow and easily propagated from sections of the trunk

The Ti Plant is widely grown in almost all the warm countries where I have been and is a staple of our house plant list. It is often confused with and sold as a Dracaena, but it is quite a different plant.

The ornamental red form is considered by the Chinese to bring good luck when it flowers. In the Philippines, the large plant in our yard flowered frequently but I cannot attest to its good luck qualities.

The most common form seen in house plant outlets is the rather broad-leaved deep red cultivar which is one of the easier house plants to grow. Use a peat-light mixture and keep it on the damp side and fertilize it regularly when the plant is actively growing.

Give the Ti Plant moderate humidity, but only mist the plant during the transition period when you bring it home from the plant shop. Constant misting will invite attacks of mealybugs, scale, and even aphids. Too low humidity should be overcome with a cold-air vaporizer instead.

The Ti Plant, especially the colored leaf forms, will take rather low light but should never be placed too far back in a room. It will do very well near a window with an eastern exposure which provides four to five hours of bright light, but of course you will not want direct sun through a window to fall on the leaves.

A common complaint is that the plant becomes tall and leggy like the common "corn" plant. There is little to be done about this; it is the nature of the plant to be tall and tree-like. If it cannot be used this way, or if it grows too tall for your room, make a number of sections of the trunk and press them sideways in a fresh pot of soil, covering one-half the trunk. Soon you will have a new plant which will be more suitable. If you have several of these sections to be rooted, fill a seed tray with a peat-light mixture and press several of these sections into the soil. It will take about a month for the roots and new sprouts to appear, at which time you should pot them for their place in the house.

Keep the leaves clean by wiping off the dust with a damp rag or giving a good dousing when watering in the bathtub or during a quick trip outside. However, do not let the leaves stay wet or you will invite insect attacks.

WANDERING JEW
Zebrina pendula

Use: Trailing pot plant or hanging basket plant
Height: 24 inches in length
Shape: Trailing
Origin: Mexico and Guatemala
Light Requirements: Medium
Humidity Requirements: Medium
Temperature Requirements: Warm
Unique Characteristics: Foolproof, easy to grow, and easy to propagate from cuttings

The Wandering Jew is well known to all house plant enthusiasts and first-year botany students. It is one of the few plants that one can recommend without hesitation to a first-time indoor plant grower because it is easy to propagate and will easily perform with only the most rudimentary knowledge.

In the deep South, where frosts are rare, it is often grown as a ground cover, which attests to its easy care.

Wandering Jew needs some good light but no direct sun through a window and should be kept on the damp side when actively growing. Fertilize also during this active growth. In the fall and winter let your plant dry a bit and water only after the surface of the soil is dry to the touch. Little fertilizer is required during this time, though I like to continue with fish oil emulsion about once a month to keep the soil in the pot lively and fertile.

Mealybugs, scale, and mites may be a problem and should be treated when seen.

Like almost all house plants, the Wandering Jew may get old, tough, and ratty-looking after a few years. I like to repot plants like this by removing the clump and choosing the younger shoots, which I then place in a new pot or basket. Some like to take a few cuttings when the plant gets old, root them, and use them as the foundation for a new pot or basket, discarding the old plant entirely.

WEEPING FIG
Ficus benjamina

Use: Tall tub plant
Height: 6 feet or more in time
Shape: Large bush or tree
Origin: India, Southeast Asia, Malaysia
Light Requirements: Moderate
Humidity Requirements: Medium
Temperature Requirements: Warm
Unique Characteristics: Strong stately plant which will easily make a tall bushy shrub-like tree or true tree

From its native habitat, the Weeping Fig has been taken throughout the world to become a standard indoor plant in the temperate and cold climates and a beautiful street or garden plant in areas of no frost or freezing temperatures. They line the streets of Cairo and Alexandria, are grown as beautiful topiaries in the most outstanding gardens of Egypt, and are found as hedge plants surrounding beautiful villas throughout that country. In Malaysia, the Weeping Fig is almost as common as a Holly in the South, being used in almost every landscaping and decorating way.

The Weeping Fig is seen everywhere indoor plants are used. Commercial buildings in need of huge indoor trees are landscaped with them. Homeowners find them lasting and satisfactory decorative plants. The Weeping Fig is easy to grow and keep beautiful inside a home if it is given the correct culture. Fortunately, these requirements are simple.

First, pot in a large enough tub or container so that repotting will not be necessary for a year or two. In other words, give it plenty of room to grow!

Second, always use a peat-light mixture which will drain well, for the death of many Weeping Figs may be directly attributed to too much water in the soil.

Third, DO NOT OVERWATER. Weeping Figs need to dry down a bit between waterings but never to the point when the soil separates from the side of the pot. Water thoroughly, letting the water run down the lower stem and into the ball of soil at the base of the stem. Water several times until the ball of soil is thoroughly wet. Allow the pot to drain until no more water is coming from the drain hole. Water again when the surface of the soil is dry to the touch.

Fourth, fertilize year-round with a soluble or liquid house plant fertilizer but reduce the strength to a maintenance level in the fall and winter.

Fifth, place your Weeping Fig in good light but not direct sun.

Sixth, do not place it near an open heat vent or in the draft of an air conditioner.

Seventh, the lack of humidity should not be a problem when it is potted in a good, light mixture and when the watering schedule is properly carried out. However, when a Weeping Fig is first brought home, it is wise to place a cold-air vaporizer nearby or mist the plant regularly as it adapts to the drier atmosphere of your home.

Eighth, scale is a Weeping Fig's most serious problem and should be attended to immediately when seen to prevent a difficult control problem from developing.

The Weeping Fig does not like to be moved around. Changes in any of the basic conditions will cause sudden and sometimes traumatic leaf drop that seems to foretell its immediate demise, which is seldom true. Complaints pour into plant shops about a new Weeping Fig which reaches its new home and suddenly sheds many of its leaves. Patience is a virtue in this case for time will quickly heal the trouble and new buds will break forth. Soon the plant seems happy as can be. In such cases the worst thing that can happen is for the new owner to change the rules and add large amounts of water or fertilizer to overcome this rather normal happening.

Betsy Hastings under pruned Weeping Fig in Malaysia

Weeping Fig in Egypt

Pruned Weeping Figs at the Marriot Hotel, Cairo

Spathyphyllum

FLOWERING HOUSEPLANTS

The plants described so far are grown primarily, though not always exclusively, for their foliage. There are Begonias which serve well as both flowering and foliage plants. The Shamrock's flowers are an added incentive to grow this interesting plant. Often a cactus or some other succulent, like the Christmas Cactus, will blossom and thrill the grower beyond belief. In fact, many tropical foliage plants will flower on occasion. However, the plants listed so far would be acceptable houseplants even if they never had any flowers.

There is another whole group of indoor plants which would seldom, if ever, be grown just for their foliage. Most of them are for devotees since they require understanding and experience, but the rewards are great when success is achieved.

Fortunately there are a number of people who have gained vast experience in growing certain of these plants, and societies abound that are dedicated to their culture. With the exception of certain Begonias described above and the Orchids which Betsy grew in Malaysia, we have never been devoted to many of these.

I have earned the somewhat dubious reputation of not liking African Violets. This came about over twenty years ago when I first started my talk-radio career. I was amazed beyond belief at the popularity of the subject of growing things. The call-in lines were constantly jammed with excellent questions and comments about gardening. The only problem was with African Violets. The African Violet devotees monopolized the lines. Most of the comments were about how pretty the caller's violets were and added precious little to the advancement of the gardening experience. My producer wanted to just cut off any caller who dwelled on the beauty of a particular violet in his window, but I just couldn't do that. So one day when a young lady called about an African Violet which was doing very poorly, I told her to take it out in the backyard and put it in the trash bin for it was a worthless plant. I soon became known as the man who hates African Violets.

I hate to admit publicly that I studied quite a bit about these plants when at Cornell and, honestly, was greatly impressed with their potential in those early days. To this day, however, I will always be known as the archenemy of African Violets.

Besides African Violets, there are a number of other specialty groups of indoor flowering plants which are exciting and fun to work with:

- Amaryllis (see bulb section)
- African Violet
- Anthurium
- Begonia (see foliage house plants)
- The Bromeliads
- Christmas Cactus (see succulents)
- Gloxinia
- Impatiens (see annual flowers)
- Ivy Geranium
- Narcissus (see bulb section)
- Orchids
- Spathiphyllum

The above list is in no way exhaustive. My mother once grew fabulous Clivia (Kaffir Lily). I have grown the Night-Blooming Cereus and felt like an idiot while sitting in front of this grubby-looking plant with a huge bud hanging down, waiting until the wee hours for the absolutely spectacular flower to open. The homes of people I know abound with the fragrance of Asiatic Jasmine. People grow Camellias inside as well as the miniature Gardenias and enjoy their wonderful blooms.

Impatiens

Betsy Hastings and her orchids, Malaysia

Ruby Pielego with one of her orchids in the Philippines

An orchid dealer in Malaysia

Under proper conditions, many outdoor plants will blossom inside. It is a matter of adjusting your indoor environment so that these outdoor plants will survive and produce the flowers you want.

To go into details about the culture of these plants would fill volumes, so I will leave it to you and the excellent societies to master the art of growing any or all of these with vast potential inside your home.

There are other plants from the warm parts of the world which are beautiful in foliage or flower but seldom perform well inside the house when central heating or air conditioning is being operated. However, many gardeners, including myself, use them outside during our warm seasons and overwinter them inside in a cool room or basement.

I do not consider these as suitable for houseplants since they are generally less than acceptable on a table or among an inside plant group. However, their spectacular flowers or unique foliage make them worthwhile on porches, patios, decks, or other outdoor living areas when the weather is warm. I discuss these plants under the heading "Inside-Outside Plants."

INSIDE-OUTSIDE PLANTS

So far, we have been thinking of growing plants inside all the time. However, there are many of us who like plants inside during the winter, yet have spots on porches, decks, and outdoor living areas where these same plants are attractive during the times of the year when there is no danger of cold weather damage.

At Sweet Apple we have an old-fashioned screened breezeway which is a wonderful spot during much of the spring, summer, and fall. In fact, we spend far more time in this outdoor living room than in our indoor one. We have found it is the perfect place for many of the houseplants which we enjoy inside during the winter. In fact, we have now developed a large group of plants as really porch plants, which must be brought inside during the winter for protection from cold.

There is another group of plants I like to grow which, as previously stated, do not fit the criteria of a houseplant for they will seldom perform well when grown inside during any season of the year. These plants are, however, a tremendous addition to the spring, summer and fall garden or outside living areas. They are generally woody plants which must be of considerable size in order to fulfill their function and are relatively expensive, which makes their use as a one-season annual a bit unrealistic for most of us. These plants are left to fulfill their function during the warm seasons and are brought inside to exist during the winter.

Many of these tropical plants are used as summer garden plants. Allamanda, single and double Hibiscus, Bougainvillea, and others are found in nurseries in the late spring. These tropical, frost-tender plants make ideal summer flowering plants when grown in pots or tubs. They are tender, however, and when purchasing you must remember they will not survive outside during the period when frost and freezing occur. They are so great an addition to the garden that they should be used despite the question of what to do with them in the winter.

The problem with most of these plants is that they are almost always plants which need high light intensity and high humidity. Thus, it is very difficult to keep them growing well under inside conditions. The best place for them is in a solarium or greenhouse where they will have a good chance to do well. Since most people do not have such a place, overwintering becomes an effort merely to keep them alive until spring, so they can be taken outside to start growing and blooming once again. They are usually best kept during the wintertime in a basement which is not too warm but never freezes and where there is light. Keep them on the dry side, but never allow them to dry completely. Though most of their leaves will fall off, this is not necessarily disastrous. Do not fertilize; if you do, the new weak and spindly growth which comes out will be of little use. Merely try to keep them alive and resting during wintertime.

Care of Inside-Outside Plants

No matter which way you look at your "inside-outside" plants—plants for a given spot outside which must be brought in during the winter in order to survive, or plants from inside which you like outside in the summer—you need to handle them in a special way.

PLACING HOUSEPLANTS OUTSIDE DURING THE SUMMER

The inside plants which you take outside in the summer must be carefully placed outside. Remember what I have said about inside light being far inferior to even a shaded spot outside. It is very easy to put inside plants into far too intense light outside, resulting in "leaf burn" and sometimes very poor growth. Never take an inside plant outside into direct sun, for you may damage or even kill it.

Use the camera experiment to check for places with light conditions similar to those from which you are taking the plants. Even though the plants may adjust to the higher light conditions in a short time, remember that in a few months you will have to reverse the procedure and bring them back inside. It is far better to match conditions between the two different places than to spend so much time adjusting back and forth.

Plants usually grow far better outside than inside. Nature is just a better provider of growing conditions than we are inside our houses. Plants outside will need more frequent fertilizing with this greater growth. During the hottest parts of the summer, especially if it is very dry, plants may need watering more frequently. Use the same watering rules described for watering plants when they are inside but be aware that the cycle may be far more frequent.

Insects and diseases are also much more of a problem when the plants are outside. Many insects will come over to your delicious house plants from other shrubs and plants in your garden or someone else's. Keep a sharp lookout all the time and treat immediately whenever you notice a problem.

Before moving plants outside, check to see if they need repotting. Growth will increase under the better conditions outside, so if you are in doubt, repot them when you move them outside.

PLACING OVERWINTERED TROPICAL PLANTS OUTSIDE

Tropical plants used as summer plants outside and which you have carried over during the winter should be readied for the move outside well ahead of the beginning of warm, cold-free outside temperatures.

Woody plants like Hibiscus, Bougainvillea, Ixora, Croton, and tropical Jasmines should be inspected and all dead twigs pruned out. Judicious pruning of the main plant structure is also advisable to force healthy young growth on which the foliage or blooms will form.

Plants which grew heavily last season should be repotted if necessary. Determine this by carefully removing the ball of earth from the pot and looking at the mat of roots against the outside of the ball. If they are heavy, dark, and thickly matted, the plant will definitely need repotting with new soil and a larger pot. (See general rules for repotting at the beginning of this section on house plants.) After pruning and repotting if necessary, set the plants in a warm, bright location. Water thoroughly and fertilize well. Try to time this so that they may be set outside as soon as the buds begin to grow.

PLACING HOUSEPLANTS INSIDE IN THE FALL

As the weather becomes cooler in September, especially at night, you should start the process of readying the plants which are to be taken back inside.

Pick up each plant and check for sowbugs and pillbugs underneath. If you see any, dust under the pot and place some of the material on the surface of the soil in the pot; then water it into the ball of soil. This will kill any of these pests which have nested in the root ball. At the same time, check for any other insects present and treat carefully. You do not wish to introduce unwanted pests to your other plants inside.

If there is appreciably more light in your outside area than where the plants will be placed inside, you must start adjusting your plants to the lesser light conditions. Move them gradually into less and less light until they are finally in light similar to that inside. Make this transition over a period of several weeks to prevent sudden shock to the plant.

The ideal time to bring plants inside is between the time your turn the air conditioning off and the time you turn the heat on. There will be a less drastic drop in the humidity differential during this time and plants will suffer far less.

Be prepared to run the cold-air vaporizer or to mist your plants frequently once they are inside. Treat them as described earlier when handling houseplants during the transition period. These plants will soon resume their beautiful indoor look and become your inside winter garden.

PLACING TROPICAL PLANTS INSIDE IN THE FALL

The best place for these plants is a conservatory like a warm greenhouse or solarium. Try to match the light conditions under which they have been growing outside. Reduce the frequency of watering and fertilize lightly just to keep them healthy.

Since most people do not have such a structure as a greenhouse or solarium, the plants must be put into a semidormant resting stage until they are readied for moving outside once again.

Bring them in earlier than you take cuttings from Geraniums, Impatiens, or Begonias, or dig Caladiums or Dahlias, for they will suffer greatly under low night temperatures. Check the soil for sowbugs and other insects just like you do for houseplants which have been outside all summer. Clean up any leaf or stem insects before you bring them inside. Give them a thorough watering and a little fertilizer the day before you bring them in.

Take them to their winter place and let them slowly dry down. Never let these plants dry completely, but do not keep them nearly as damp as when they are growing. Keep them on the cool side but certainly not cold. You are trying to make them stop their growth and rest for a while.

ALL ABOUT INSIDE-OUTSIDE PLANTS

ALLAMANDA
Allamanda cathartica, various cultivars

Though originally from South America, this plant is seen all over the world because in its bushy form (the species is a tall climber), it is one of the most colorful and free-blooming shrubs of the tropics.

It is a bit difficult to overwinter but the results make the extra effort worthwhile. Keep it in a bright, not too cool spot, and do not let it dry completely. Prune back heavily prior to putting it back outside.

Outside they are best grown in a large tub in bright sun. Give them heavy waterings, and do not let the soil dry out. Fertilize twice a month with a soluble or liquid fertilizer at full rate. If you keep the fresh growth nipped back, they will remain dense and bushy, setting huge numbers of bright yellow flowers.

BANANA
Musa acuminata

In the house plant list I covered how to grow a Banana inside the home. This unusual and typically tropical-appearing plant will add a great deal to any inside plantings.

The Banana is also an excellent tub plant for porches, patios, and other outdoor living areas. The Dwarf Cavendish cultivar is the best for this purpose due to its maximum height of ten to twelve feet. When grown in a large tub outside they are very difficult to move inside due to the size and weight of the pot, and seldom will the plant adjust well enough to be attractive during the winter in one of your living rooms.

You can avoid this problem by overwintering the huge plant in a semi-dormant resting state. When the first frosty weather arrives, remove the Banana from the pot, leaving as much soil around the roots as possible. Wrap the root ball in a plastic garbage bag and tie around the base of the stem. Place the Banana on its side in a cool but never freezing spot such as a basement with windows. Do not remove the stems or leaves. In the spring when the danger of frost has passed, cut off the top about twelve to eighteen inches above the roots. Repot in your big outside tub using fresh peat-light soil. (See Banana in the houseplant list for details of potting.)

Your Banana will survive for many years in this manner and will have a good chance of flowering and fruiting. Remember that a Banana flowers and fruits on a stalk only once. When your plant fruits, treat the plant the same except the following spring you should find a side sprout to repot rather than the old mother plant.

Years ago there was an adventurous gardener in southwest Atlanta who devised another system for growing his Banana year after year. During the summer he had this fine plant growing in his front yard and people would drive by to see the

Allamanda

Allamanda

Double Bougainvillea in Malaysia

Bougainvillea, Philippines

Double red Bougainvillea

unbelievable sight. Surely, the Georgia winters should finish off this plant, but every summer it stood there as happy as if it were in Costa Rica or the Philippines.

His secret was that he never dug up this plant but each winter he would cut it off about eighteen inches to two feet above the ground and build an old-fashioned sweet potato hill over it. First he would make a teepee out of some type of canes, leaving plenty of air space around the main Banana stalk. Next he would place a heavy layer of sod on the outside of the teepee to insulate the plant still standing inside. There the Banana lived, just like sweet potatoes live, for the entire frigid winter. When frost danger had passed, the hill was removed and the Banana would sprout forth in a great rush to adorn his landscape. One year he called and we went by to see a huge cluster of fruit.

This hybrid system was obviously derived from his early life in the Georgia countryside where food was so scarce that sweet potatoes had to be carried over the winter for a family to remain well-fed. Since sweet potatoes are not frost-hardy, just like the Banana, this gardener surmised that this would be a perfect way to keep his prize plant alive in the yard. The sight of a large hill in the yard during the winter didn't seem to bother him or the rest of us who waited anxiously for his Banana to pop up each spring.

BOUGAINVILLEA
Bougainvillea X

These spectacular vines originally came from South America, but I have seen them growing in almost every tropical country to which I have traveled. They have been hybridized over and over, and now there are cultivars of many colors as well as singles and doubles.

Bougainvilleas are grown in the tropics and in greenhouses as vines or as a bush. I have seen them growing as trellis covers in the Philippines, and we had pots of them pruned as bushes in front of our home in Kuala Lumpur. The most beautiful plantings I have ever seen were in the northern part of Morocco where they lined the entrance to a project on which I worked for a while. These massive plants were pruned into a shrub which stood over eight feet tall and was at least six feet across.

In the tropics, they bloom most of the time but have the greatest bloom after a dry spell has broken and the rains come. Some cultivars seem to have the heaviest blooms during periods of drought, however.

The easiest way to grow the Bougainvillea as both an inside and outside plant is to keep it bushy by constantly pruning off the runners.

Outside, water thoroughly, but let the surface of the soil be dry to the touch before rewatering. Inside, keep on the dry side all the time. A good watering twice a month should be sufficient. Fertilize each time you water during the winter but mix the solution at one-half strength.

During the winter, it will lose a tremendous number of leaves, but don't despair. The warmth of spring and relocation outside will quickly return this lovely plant to health and vigor.

CROTON
Codiaeum variegatum

This native of the Malay Peninsula and some of the Pacific islands has spread far and wide and is grown outside in the frost-free southern United States and inside in greenhouses. The number of leaf forms is extraordinarily high, from broadleaf forms to very lacy and narrow forms. The colors are also broad-ranged, with mixtures of yellows, reds, greens, and purples predominating.

The Croton is not a good houseplant because it requires bright sun for best coloring and high humidity for good growth. It is therefore a plant for the summer patio, deck, or garden spot where it performs very well in tropical splendor.

The difficulty is carrying over the Croton; unlike the Hibiscus Rosa-sinensis and the Allamanda, it doesn't seem to need or want a resting period. Thus winter storage is difficult at best. The easiest way to keep it is to place it in a moderately warm place and in as much light as possible without direct sun through the window (except perhaps in the morning). Misting will help somewhat, but do not expect it to look all that good during the winter. Keep it watered about the same as your tropical plants (like Philodendrons), but do not overwater.

If excessive leaf fall occurs, leave the plant alone until spring, cut back into good, lively wood, repot if necessary, fertilize, water, and put outside where it will be happy.

RED GINGER
Alpinia purpurata

The Red Ginger is certainly not a common plant found in nurseries in the South, although it should be. The culture is simple and it grows and blooms quickly after reviving outside in the late spring.

Plant the Red Ginger in a large, 12-inch or more pot or tub, and it will quickly make a huge plant filled with the highly unusual red flowers. Give it plenty of sun, water, and fertilizer when it is actively growing.

In the early fall, bring it inside to a well-lighted, cool place, and keep relatively dry during the winter. Cut it back in March; water thoroughly and fertilize heavily.

When the temperature is warm, place it outside in a sunny spot for another summer filled with exciting blossoms.

HIBISCUS
Hibiscus Rosa–sinensis, many cultivars

In almost every tropical part of the world and even in South Florida, the Hibiscus is grown for its beautiful form and spectacular blossoms. They are used as garden plants, hedges, and tub plants. The color range is extremely broad and the flower form varies from large singles with protruding anthers to huge doubles.

This Hibiscus is not the same as our other commonly-grown forms, althea *H. Syriacus* and mallows (hardy perennial Hibiscus), and the gardener should be

Crotons growing in a solarium in Dallas, Texas

Red Ginger

Hibiscus, the rose of the tropics

Red Ginger

Single Hibiscus

Double red Hibiscus

Double Salmon Hibiscus

A gorgeous single Hibiscus

Large leaf Ixora, seldom
grown in the United States

Ixora

aware of this plant's ability to withstand cold. This tropical Hibiscus is so beautiful that it should still be used as a tub plant outside during the summer and given proper protection and treatment during the winter.

It is not suitable as a houseplant, for the dim environment and dry atmosphere will prevent it from performing well. It is possible to grow it to great advantage outside during the warm seasons and overwinter it in a semiresting state during the winter.

Follow the general rules for handling this type of plant but cut it back more severely each spring before resetting it outside. The *Hibiscus Rosa-sinensis* is a heavy feeder and will need weekly fertilizing with a soluble fertilizer when it is growing profusely during the summer. Grow it in the full sun for best results and keep it well-watered. Tip pruning is also advantageous and keeps the plant bushy as well as forcing growth on which the blossoms are formed.

Watch for insects on your Hibiscus. There is a small worm which devastates all Hibiscus foliage, but a spray of bacillus thuringiensis (BT) is an excellent control. Though aphids and thrips may also be problems, they are easily controlled with a good garden spray.

The Hibiscus is easy to root from young stem cuttings. Take these in the late summer when the plant is actively growing and root in damp perlite. Use wood which has come out recently but has hardened up.

 IXORA
Ixora coccinea

The *Ixora coccinea* is but one of the several Ixoras which I encountered in the Philippines and Malaysia. There are tall, large-leaf species (*Ixora javanica* is one) which are widely grown for the larger shrub and heavier heads of flowers.

The Ixora which we see here in the United States is the *I. coccinea,* also widely found in tropical countries. It is most often used in these warm areas as hedges or large groupings in the garden. It does well in pots, and many homes in Malaysia have them growing in brightly-lighted places.

Our use of the Ixora is generally as a tub specimen plant where, after a few years of good growth and frequent trimming, it becomes a thick shrub with a covering of the orange-red flowers.

Ixoras, like the Crotons, are not happy with the low light and dry air of our homes in the winter. Treat them the same way as the Croton and hope for the best. Summer rejuvenation, however, is quick and the plant will soon be beautiful once again.

OTHER INSIDE-OUTSIDE PLANTS

There are many more tropical plants with which you may have good results using the general inside-outside techniques described above. They really add a tremendous amount of interest to the garden, outdoor living area, or patio and should be tried on a limited basis as you perfect the technique of overwintering.

INDEX

Tropical houseplants, **105**, 108–120
Tying, of plants, 12
Tuberose: *Polianthes tuberosa,* 77, **78**
Tuberous-rooted begonias, 143
Tulip: *Tulipa* sp., **61**, 77–79, **78, 79**

Vinca: *Catharanthus roseus,* **xv, 6**, 43
Vines, 85–101, *see also specific types*
  herbaceous, 98–101
  woody, 89–97
Viola X wittrockiana, see Pansy
Violets, African *see* African Violets
Virginia Creeper: *Parthenocissus*
  quinquefolia, 96–97
Vitis sp., *see* Grape

Wandering Jew: *Zebrina pendula,* 200
Water breaker, **11**
Watering
  ferns, 155
  flower garden, 11
  houseplants, 124, 131–134

Wax Begonia: *Begonia X*
  semperflorens-cultorum, 18, **19**
Weeping Fig: *Ficus benjamina,* **200**,
  201–202
White Periwinkle, **39**
Wine Lily, **81**
Wisteria: *Wisteria* sp., **94**, 97
Wisteria floribunda, see Japanese
  Wisteria
Wisteria sinensis, see Chinese Wisteria
Woody vines, 89–97

X Fatshedera Lizei, see Fatshedera

Yellow Calla Lily, **81**

Zantedeschia aethiopica, see Calla Lily
Zebrina pendula, see Wandering Jew
Zephyranthes sp., *see* Fairy Lily; Rain
  Lily
Zinnia: *Zinnia elegans,* 43, **43**